GLOSSARY OF TRANSFORMATIONAL GRAMMAR

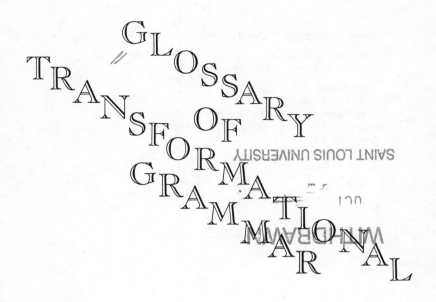

GLOSSARY OF TRANSFORMATIONAL GRAMMAR

Jeanne Ambrose-Grillet
University of Massachusetts, Boston

NEWBURY HOUSE PUBLISHERS, INC. / ROWLEY / MASS.

Library of Congress Cataloging in Publication Data

Ambrose-Grillet, Jeanne.
  Glossary of transformational grammar.

  Bibliography: p.
  Includes index.
  1. Generative grammar--Terminology. I. Title.
P158.A4   415   78-1819
ISBN 0-88377-099-7

Cover design by Barbara Frake.

NEWBURY HOUSE PUBLISHERS, INC.

Language Science
Language Teaching
Language Learning

ROWLEY, MASSACHUSETTS 01969

First printing: August 1978
          5   4   3   2

Printed in the U.S.A.

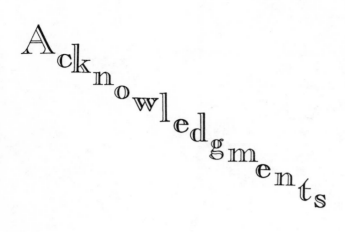

Acknowledgments

This book began as a collection of notes done as exercises when I first tried to read the linguistic works of Noam Chomsky. Later I began to feel that it might help others whose curiosity led them to delve into the subject of transformational grammar. I began to write down the content of the Glossary in a more careful manner and then with the help and questioning of many of my students, friends, and fellow teachers formulated this book. I thank them all for their invaluable comments. I am especially indebted to Noam Chomsky, Morris Halle and David Perlmutter who generously allowed me to attend their classes at Massachusetts Institute of Technology and gave me the great privilege of seeing linguistics "in the making."

This work was supported in part by a grant from the University of Massachusetts in Boston and their assistance is gratefully acknowledged.

Jeanne Ambrose-Grillet

Contents

Historical Background

Jeffrey L. Houben
University of Massachusetts, Boston

WHY COMPOSE A GLOSSARY?

Among the earliest documents "written on clay" that have been discovered in the Middle East are numerous bilingual glossaries. The recently unearthed tablets from Ebla in Syria are no exception. Word lists, general or specialized, facilitated accurate interpretation of hallowed Sumerian texts by successor Semitic and Indo-European speech communities. A similar need now exists. With the rapid growth in technology and analysis there has come a corresponding flood of jargon, the specialized terminology invented or adapted by the members of new discipline-communities. The science of linguistics in particular has produced a rapid succession of "terminological generations," each aiming at the most accurate expression of the latest conception of language and its accompanying phenomena. This glossary by Jeanne Ambrose-Grillet, then, is a contemporary contribution to an enterprise as ancient as written language itself. The vocabulary of one burgeoning field of linguistic knowledge, the post-1957, Chomskyan study of syntax, is without doubt idiomatic enough to call for a descriptive and definitive glossary.

LANGUAGE ABOUT LANGUAGE

A linguistic glossary is an extraordinary example of the genre because its goal is to characterize language in and by language. The vocabulary of linguistic description is at once part of a particular language and independent of it; its referent is an item or process of the system it is itself using. Insofar as a linguistic term is part of a language, it is bound by the rules and changes that the entire language undergoes, especially in the area of semantic extension. A specific element in a technical vocabulary may also be used in everyday speech. In the process its technical significance is blurred and a new term is introduced by specialists. For example, because the word *subject* has gradually come to mean "topic" in common English, an unavoidable confusion has resulted in the understanding of the grammatical term *subject*. Thus, those taught to identify the *subject* of a sentence need the assistance of a special glossary to cope with a contemporary refinement: "the NP which is directly dominated by S" (p. 90). Similarly, a term may outlive its technical usefulness because the type of linguistic description for which it was created has been abandoned. A case in point is the phrase *to parse* a sentence, in which the verb is derived from the Latin noun *pars* (*orationis*) = "part of speech." Both the term and traditional grammatical drills have fallen into disuse. The obsolescence of the phrase *objective case* may soon follow owing to the current adjectival usage (an *objective* statement) and to the trend away from Latin and grammatical analyses based on it. At any rate, it is important to distinguish between the world of scientific linguistic analysis and the world of "language use," precisely because the former can be expressed only by the latter. To this end specialists develop a *metalanguage* which has conventions (diacritics, formalisms) to bridge the gap between normal expression and technical comments about language structure. It will also contain apparent violations of standard language as written or spoken by laymen.

Metalanguage needs terms or symbols to describe various aspects and levels of grammatical segments (of words, sentences, etc.) rather than merely to make semantic distinctions. Special brackets and algebraic symbols are commonly used as shorthand markers of linguistic processes or operations. For instance, in this volume curly brackets represent alternate choices, arrows indicate grammatical restructuring or the effect of phonological environment, and technical abbreviations designate abstractions of linguistic or theoretical units. Thus, the words "might be expressed" used below can be called a *constituent of VP* (= *verb phrase*) in the current metalanguage or the pronunciation of a word might be expressed as a grid of plus and minus features! New verbs, nouns, and adjectives are created to cover postulated grammatical and psychological processes: *map*, to project symbols from one level to another; *cognize*, to display a native speaker's intuitive knowledge of his language; *homonymity*, the situation in which one sentence has different "readings"; *sortal*, descriptive of a group of objects sharing certain properties. A term of metalanguage can also group linguistic entities of differing status (syllable, morpheme, word, grammatical category) in order to show parallel grammatical treatment. Thus, the syllabic boundary symbol #, the suffixes *-ic*, *-ion*, and the category of past tense may all be called *grammatical formatives*. Finally, a process typified by the behavior of one word will sometimes be dubbed by a phrase which generalizes the very process: *EACH-movement, RAISING*. These terms will then be transferred even to foreign-language description when applicable, thereby becoming still more abstract and more obviously metalinguistic.

Metalanguage is not an exclusively modern phenomenon. Like any language it has undergone and is undergoing change. However, this change is not the result of internal development and transmission alone. It is tied to the contemporary perspective on language, its parts, and processes. The mathematical and philosophical bent of current linguistic terminology as seen in this glossary reflects not only two preëminent modern modes of inquiry, computerized study and formal logic, but also the basis for and scope of that inquiry, namely, linguistic universals and the relation of language to cognition. Simply stated, linguistic thought is crystallized and even fossilized in linguistic terminology, as a glance at the development and use of some technical terms will reveal.

SEVERAL PERIODS OF WESTERN METALINGUISTIC TRADITION

In the "beginning" of Western linguistic analysis was the Indo-European "word." Both its root and meaning are found in the Latin (*verbum*) and Gothic (*waurds*) cognates of our English lexeme *word*. This is the only word recoverable from the pre-historic "linguistic" vocabulary of our language family, and it is remarkable that this form has, from high antiquity, remained so semantically stable in Europe. Its connection with a recon-structed root *wer-* "to speak" allows us to assume that it was created in a preliterate society.

In contrast to this modest start, the Greeks coined dozens of metalinguistic terms in the 4th century B.C. One that has proven most durable is *suzugia* ("together-yoke-hood") which the Romans calqued (= translated literally) as *conjugatio*. But it is clear that the Greeks did not restrict the use of *suzugia* to verbs as later Roman grammarians did. No one is certain of the steps in the metaphorical transfer of meaning from an obviously rustic to a metalinguistic setting. But, when Plato and Aristotle used this term it already had a technical meaning. At this stage *suzugia* could refer to a pair of extremes in an on-going process or to the linkage of similar items: waking and sleeping, living and dying (Plato *Phaedo*); hot and cold, dry and wet (Aristotle *Meteorologica*). Later the term applied to the shared parts of larger word units. Cicero (*Topica*) uses the Greek convention and lists *sapiens, sapientia, sapienter* as a *conjugatio*, based on the shared root: *sapient-*. Thus, later Roman grammarians—and contemporary students of Latin—*conjugate* the verb "to love" *am-o, am-as, am-at*, etc.

The modern English word *syntax* was borrowed c. 1600 directly from Greek, where it originally meant a "marshaling of troops" and later a "combination of words." In current linguistics it refers to the base of a language's grammar and especially to the rules governing sentence-structure. A Roman borrowing of the same Greek word brought it into our meta-language again during this period in the Latin technical phrase (*grammatical*) *construction*. Perhaps the Romans found an architectural rather than military analogy in the term. Modern schoolteachers' comments about English usage seem to reflect such an image: "weak" and "balanced" constructions, "parallel" structures, "broken" English, sentence "fragments."

Curiously, the French word *grammaire* has two descendants in English ultimately due to the medieval curriculum which included the *ars grammatica* (the title of Donatus' Latin textbook, 4th century A.D.). This was originally a technical term for the "skill of writing (correctly)" and was true to its Greek origin in the root *graph-* "to write." It seems, however, that it came to be synonymous with the study of Latin and the occult texts reserved for those who could read. (The connotation of *ars* = "skill" which extended to magical as well as liberal arts probably abetted the development.) A double usage of the Old French *gramaire* (sic) arose. The net result in English is both *glamor* (the magical quality) and *grammar* (the compositional skill). Witness Robert Burns' combination:

> "Ye gipsy-gang that deal in glamor,
> And you deep read in hell's black grammar,
> Warlocks and witches." (c. 1789)

The moral is that metalanguage can not only gain currency, travel, and build analogies, but also mislead in the process. Therefore, it must constantly be renewed by supplement and redefinition.

In the modern age language study has again drawn on learned research as a model for its terminology and analysis. The gifted linguist de Saussure shows the influence of mathematics and science in his epoch-making article, "Mémoire sur le système primitif des voyelles dans les langues indo-européennes" (1879). His procedure is unmistakably algebraic because he is postulating the existence of lost sounds ("unknowns") that left traces in roots of various Indo-European languages. He conventionally symbolizes them by letters and inserts them into verbal proportions analogous to mathematical ratios. In this way he successfully explains several types of irregularity and can partially identify the lost sounds. The name he assigns them is "coefficient sonantique." With this term he recalls the coefficients of mathematical and scientific formulas in his reconstructions of prehistoric sounds.

Lastly, de Saussure utilizes the new term *phoneme* (built on Greek *phone*, "voice, sound," plus *-(e)ma*, a noun suffix) for a prime unit of sound. The word was later to become the model on which many other linguistic terms were built: morpheme, tagmeme, sememe, lexeme. In this connection it is difficult to ignore the 19th and early 20th century penchant for identifying and naming basic scientific structural units with Greek and Latin roots: nucleus, electron, proton, photon, elements of the periodic table.

De Saussure's youthful article anticipates the express aim of 20th century scholars: to abandon the traditional approach to language studies and so delineate linguistics as an independent scientific discipline. Terminological repercussions followed, especially in the United States. The traditional terms *philology; tenues, mediae,* and *aspiratae* (famous classes of sounds in Indo-European studies); *part of speech; word*; and even *sentence* were formally rejected. The latter two, for example, were replaced with the analytic and non-connotative terms *morpheme* and *utterance.* Such principles as the *complementarity of phonemic distribution* or the *biuniqueness of phonemes* give terminological evidence of the abstract, structuralist approach to language. Moreover, the use of this new vocabulary itself prevented the backsliding of linguists into patterns of thought or methods infected by traditional, "Latinate" grammatical studies. Research shifted instead to the isolation of axiomatic, symbolic, and universal linguistic truths much as pure science seeks universal principles and ideally expresses them in mathematical formulas. Therefore, the terms and phrases in this volume reflect a mature field indebted to computer studies (a *model* of language, the phonological *component, generative* grammar), mathematics (*transformational* and *recursive* rules), information theory (*redundancy* rules), and logic (*quantifier*-placement). These expressions are no longer programmatic devices for the guidance of research, but the signposts of successful and on-going scientific activity and achievement.

Two final comments. Modern linguists have already created a new methodology which is useful not only in linguistics but also in other disciplines. To indicate the breadth of the new trends, we mention the title of Levi-Strauss' first publication, "L'analyse structurale en linguistique et en anthropologie," and of Nagler's article on Greek epic poetry, "Towards a Generative View of the Homeric Formula." Or, there is the transfer of the computer metaphor via linguistics to the ethnographic *conscious model* of a culture in the minds of its members, a concept comparable to the Chomskyan linguistic notion of a native speaker's *competence*. Better known, if less rigorous, is Bernstein's recent application of linguistic terms to musical analysis:

"Similarly, . . . we found new ambiguities in Mozart's G-minor Symphony, . . . arising from violated symmetry, deep-structure symmetries which were converted by linguistic transformational procedures into beautifully ambiguous surface structures." (*The Unanswered Question*, p. 197)

But terminology is more than an index of attainment and fresh activity. It is also the creator of disputes. Linguistics as much as any other discipline is open to such difficulties. (Two instructive instances can be found in the articles of Hill and Bar-Hillel, noted contemporary linguists, that are addressed to terminological disagreements in the second volume of *Foundations of Language* [1966].) This glossary aims not simply to be a catalogue, but to prevent such unfortunate, time- and energy-wasting misunderstanding.

Introduction

This Glossary is an attempt to provide students, teachers and other interested people with a tool which will help them proceed through the work of Noam Chomsky and other linguists who write in the field of transformational grammar.

There has been a growing interest in linguistics in the past years, but many new students are not well equipped to read the literature because of the technical terminology.

Our Glossary is intended for students who have little or no background in linguistics and for those taking an introductory course in transformational linguistics. We try to explain the basic concepts used by Chomsky and other linguists of the same school.

The concepts are listed by alphabetical order. Each term is defined in Chomsky's own words whenever possible, or by a paraphrase of a text by Chomsky, with a reference indicating the source. The definitions also trace the development of Chomsky's theory, from *Syntactic Structures* (1957) to *Reflections on Language* (1975). We have based this book essentially on Chomsky's work because of his outstanding position in this part of linguistics.

The Glossary is followed by an Appendix explaining the basic transformations. This is accompanied by a bibliography with references to various controversial issues.

List of Symbols

ϕ empty set (This is used to note the possibility of having nothing in the indicated place.)

( )   parentheses indicate the optionality of the symbol or symbols within the parentheses

{ }   braces are used to abbreviate two or more rules. The elements within the braces exclude each other.

[ ]   square brackets can be used to indicate the features. (They are also used with subscript symbols to indicate that the element or elements within are dominated by the subscript symbol.)

→	the simple arrow means: "rewrite as"
⇒	the double arrow indicates a structural change
+	plus sign is the symbol of concatenation. It also indicates formative boundary. Within square brackets + and − indicate value + or − of the features
#	a double cross indicates word boundary or string boundary
/	slash means "in the environment"
/ /	two slashes indicate a phoneme
*	unacceptable
‾	a bar above a symbol indicates that this symbol dominates another symbol belonging to the same category
α	a variable
Adj	adjective
Art	article

Aux   auxiliary

β a variable

C   a consonant (C also indicates concord or agreement.)

C_0 C sub zero indicates a string of zero or more consonants

COMP   complementizer

CS   complex symbols

DS   deep structure

Δ dummy element representing any category

Det   determiner

-en   affix representing the past participle

F   a set of instruction formulas

G   a grammar

-ing	affix representing the present participle
IPM	initial phrase-marker
L	a language, or a linguistic level
M	modal (*will, can*, etc.)
N	noun
NP	noun phrase
P-marker	phrase-marker
PP	prepositional phrase
Pro	pronoun
Prt	particle
PSG	phrase-structure grammar
Refl	reflexive
S or Σ	sentence

SC	structural change
SD	structural description
SI	semantic interpretation
SR	semantic representation
SS	surface structure
T	transformation
Tns	tense
V	verb, or vowel
VP	verb phrase
Φ	mapping
WH	words such as *which* or *what*
W, X, Y, Z	variables

GLOSSARY

A-OVER-A PRINCIPLE

The A-over-A principle, proposed by Chomsky, is a postulated *universal* which constitutes an empirical claim about the structure of human language; it is an empirical hypothesis which states that "if the phrase X of *category* A is *embedded* within a larger phrase ZXW which is also of category A, then no rule applying to the category A applies to X but only to ZXW." (Chomsky, 1964a: 930-931)

In other words, given two phrases, one *dominating* the other and both of the same category, there is no *transformation* in the   grammar which can apply independently to the dominated phrase. We will give here only one of the illustrations of this principle:

Mary chased

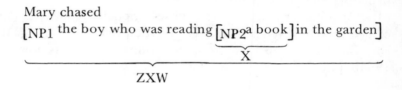

The question transformation which consists in replacing a *NP* by *WH* and moving it to the front of a string can only apply to NP1: Who(m) did Mary chase who was reading a book in the garden? NP2 cannot be submitted to a question transformation: *What did Mary chase the boy who was reading in the garden?

For discussion of this principle see Chomsky (1973), (1974a), and Ross (1967).

ADEQUACY

(a) "A grammar is descriptively adequate to the extent that it correctly describes the intrinsic *competence* of the idealized native speaker." **Descriptive adequacy** corresponds to the linguistic *intuition*—the tacit competence—of the native speaker.

In this sense, the grammar is justified on external grounds. A linguistic theory that is concerned only with descriptive adequacy does not go beyond *structural description*. (Chomsky, 1965, p. 24, 27, 34)

(b) A grammar meets the condition of **explanatory adequacy** if it offers an explanation for the intuition of the native speaker. The level of explanatory adequacy is much deeper, for it must justify the grammar on internal grounds, on grounds of its relation to a linguistic theory that constitutes an explanatory hypothesis about the form of language as such. The attempt to achieve explanatory adequacy is identical to the attempt to discover *linguistic universals*. (Chomsky, 1965, p. 27, 36)

(c) **Empirical adequacy** is a loose term which simply implies that the utterance coincides with, and is justified by, the experience of the speaker. One aspect of empirical adequacy is explanatory adequacy. (Chomsky, 1974)

(d) "A grammar that aims for **observational adequacy** is concerned merely to give an account of the primary data (e.g. the corpus) that is the input to the learning device." (Chomsky, 1964b, p. 63)

ADJUNCTION

A node B is the sister of a node C if B and C are dominated by the same node A. B and C are said to be **sister-adjoined.**

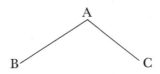

The operation called **Chomsky-adjunction** involves the copy of node A above the initial node A and the creation of a new node which allows the insertion of a new element. This new node remains unlabelled. This device was first used in

Chomsky (1957) for the introduction of *by* in the passive transformation.

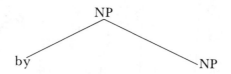

ALPHABET

Chomsky uses the expression "**alphabet** of a language" to refer to the vocabulary of a language. "The alphabet of a language is the finite set of symbols out of which its sentences are constructed . . . A language is defined by giving its alphabet and its grammatical sentences." (Chomsky, 1957:21)

AMBIGUITY

Ambiguity can be the result of:

(a) *phonological homonymy*, ex: The book was *read*.
                                                  The book was *red*.

(b) *lexical homonymy*, ex: He is going to the *bank*. (either the place of business or a place by the side of a river)

(c) *constructional homonymy*, that is to say, two or more *syntactic descriptions* can be assigned to a sentence, ex: old men and women can be read either as (old men) and (women) or as (old men) and (old women).

ANALYZABILITY

A *string* can be represented by a *tree* which can be **analyzed** (or factored) into *constituents*. For example, the string:

The boy will eat the cake

has the structure represented by the following tree:

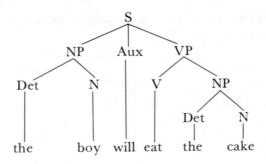

This can be properly analyzed as:

S
NP Aux VP
NP Aux V NP
Det N Aux V NP
etc. . . .

A string is properly analyzed only if each of its *terminal elements* is *dominated* by a *nonterminal symbol* which is expressed, in the same exact unbroken order, in the *structural description* (SD) of the rule which is going to apply. The passive rule optionally applies only to structures in which the unbroken sequence NP Aux V NP can be isolated (NP Aux V or Aux VP does not meet the structural analysis [or structural description] of that string) and is identical to the structural analysis required by that *transformational rule*.

The symbol of the SD is written as a product where it is understood that the successive elements in the chain are to be connected by "and" and "or." Because a Boolean algebra is, by definition, an algebraic system in which "and" and "or" are the essential operations, these are called **Boolean Conditions on Analyzability.** For example, the structural description of negative insertion is:

$$NP - Tense(\begin{Bmatrix} Modal \\ Have \\ Be \end{Bmatrix}) - V$$

It will read: noun-phrase and tense and (nothing or modal or *have* or *be*) and verb.

ANAPHORA

Traditionally, **anaphora** means "the repetition of the same word or phrase in several successive clauses." (Oxford English Dictionary) Chomsky uses the term in a broader sense, to indicate a co-referential situation. In a structure of the form: NP . . . one another, ex: John's parents hate one another, *John's parents* and *one another* are anaphorically related. Chomsky suggests that anaphora is one aspect of *semantic representation* and is determined by *surface structure*. (Chomsky, 1974)

From anaphora, which expresses a relation, Chomsky coins the word **anaphor**, which represents the agent, i.e., the element which is controlled by the antecedent NP. The anaphor may be (a) *bound* as in "John lost his way"; the anaphor *his* necessarily refers to *John*, or (b) *unbound* as in "John found his book," where *his* may refer to *John* or any other male. An anaphor can also be called an anaphoric expression, such as in the case of *each other*. (Chomsky, 1975c: 104-112)

ARCHI-SEGMENT

The Prague School coined the word *archiphoneme* to refer to all the *distinctive features* common to two phonemes in a position of neutralization. Chomsky and Halle use the term **archi-segment** to designate a segment not fully specified in terms of features, that is to say, where redundant features are omitted in order to have the most general description. *Phonological matrices* typically consist of archi-segments. (Chomsky and Halle, 1968: 166)

ASSIMILATION/DISSIMILATION

Assimilation and **dissimilation** are two terms widely used in phonology. Assimilation describes the process by which a *segment* acquires one or several characteristics belonging to a preceding or following segment.

"A nonnasal consonant becomes voiced before a voiced nonnasal (true) consonant and unvoiced before an unvoiced nonnasal consonant."

$$
\begin{bmatrix} +\text{cons} \\ -\text{voc} \\ -\text{nasal} \end{bmatrix} \longrightarrow \begin{bmatrix} \alpha\,\text{voice} \end{bmatrix} \Big/ \underline{\quad} \begin{bmatrix} +\text{cons} \\ -\text{voc} \\ -\text{nasal} \\ \alpha\,\text{voice} \end{bmatrix}
$$

(Chomsky and Halle, 1968: 178)

An example of assimilation may be found in some dialects of French in the word *médecin* "medical doctor,"where the *d* becomes unvoiced on account of the following *s* and the word is pronounced [mets ẽ].

Dissimilation describes the opposite process, to wit, a segment acquires one or several characteristics which tend to differentiate it from a segment which precedes or follows. "The first of two nonnasal (true) consonants becomes voiced where the second is unvoiced and unvoiced where the second is voiced." (Chomsky and Halle, 1968: 178)

"An example of dissimilation is found in Gothic, where, after an unstressed vowel, voicing in continuants dissimilates with that in the preceding obstruent. Thus we find *agisa* "fight," instead of *agiza.*" (Chomsky and Halle, 1968: 351)

AUXILIARY (AUX)

In a *rewriting rule* **Aux** stands for **Auxiliary** and represents a grammatical *category*. In English auxiliaries can be represented according to the case as: have+en (*have*+past participle), be+ing (*be*+present participle), be+en (*be*+past participle), or one of the modals (M), *can, must, will* etc. The phrase-structure rule for the auxiliary is:

Aux → Tense (Modal) (have) (be)

It indicates: (1) the tense of the auxiliary (present or past)
              (2) the order in which each element may occur
              (3) the optionality of the elements which are in
                  parentheses

The sentence "John must have been working" will be represented:

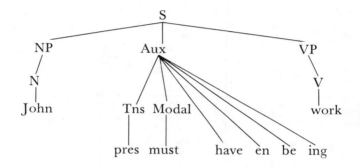

B

BASE

The *syntactic component* consists of "two systems of rules: the
base and the *transformational component* of the syntax. The
base system, or base component, is further divided into two
parts: the *categorial system* and the *lexicon*." (Chomsky,
1972a:140)

"The base of the syntactic component is a system of rules
that *generate* a highly restricted (perhaps finite) set of *basic
strings,* each with an associated structural description called a
base Phrase-marker." (Chomsky, 1965:17)

Base rules are found in the base component. They are the rewriting rules which can be divided into (a) **branching rules** of the type S → NP Predicate-Phrase and (b) *subcategorization rules* of the type V →CS which are themselves subdivided into *strict subcategorization rules* and *selectional rules.* (Chomsky, 1965:106-113)

The **base structure** (underlying or *deep structure*) is the structure to which transformations apply. Example of a base structure on which *Affix-hopping* must apply:

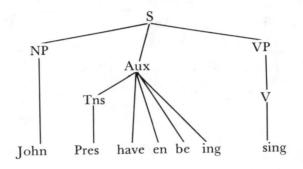

The derived sentence is: John has been singing.

BINDING

The term is due to Ross who states that a rule is "upward **bounded** if elements moved by that rule cannot be moved over this boundary (the boundary of the sentence)." (Ross, 1967: 162) A movement is **unbounded** if nothing prevents that movement from taking place.

A **binding** relation is a relation between an antecedent and its pronoun or an antecedent and its *trace*. The pronoun and the trace are bound (or controlled) by their antecedents. (Chomsky, 1975c: 92, 94, 96)

(See "Anaphor, bound and unbound.")

BOUNDARY (JUNCTURE)

A **boundary** is a sign which indicates the beginning and the end of a *formative,* a *word,* a phrase or a sentence." The + symbols represent formative boundaries which, by convention, automatically mark the beginning and end of each formative." (Chomsky and Halle, 1968:9)

The boundary # is automatically inserted at the beginning and at the end of every *string dominated* by a *major category*, i.e., by one of the *lexical categories* "noun," "verb," "adjective," or by a category such as "sentence," "noun phrase," "verb phrase," which dominates a lexical category. (Chomsky and Halle, 1968: 366)

Example:

#we##establish#past##tele + graph#ic##communicate#ion#

BRACKETING/LABELLED BRACKETING

It seems that **bracketing** was first practiced by Rulon S. Wells in order to represent a sentence. Bloch and Harris extended the use of the brackets, giving each bracket the name of its syntactic class. This **labelled bracketing** represents the *structural description* of a sentence. The sentence "We established telegraphic communication" will be bracketed in the following manner:

**[S[NP[N +we+]N]NP][VP[V[V+establish+] V+past+]
V[NP[A[N+tele+[STEM+ graph+]STEM]N +ic+]A[
N[V+communicate+] V +ion+]N]NP]VP]S**

(Chomsky and Halle, 1968:7-9)

A **primitive labelled bracketing** is the bracketing of a *kernel sentence*.

BRANCHING

Branching is the analysis of a *category* into a sequence of categories, as when S is analyzed into NPAuxVP or NP into DetN.

A **branching rule** analyzes a category symbol into a *string* of (one or more) symbols, each of which is either a *terminal* *symbol* or a nonterminal category. The branching rules are those rules of the form A→Z/X—W (X and W may be zero) in which neither A nor Z involves any *complex symbols*. Ex: S→NPPredicate-Phrase, or Aux→Tense (M)

A **multiple branching construction** has the form

$$\big[[A]\,[B]\,\ldots\,[M]\big]$$

A **left-branching structure** has the form:

$$\Big[\big[[\cdots\cdots]\cdots\big]\cdots\Big]\text{——————}$$

Ex: Quite a few of the students whom you met who come from New York are friends of mine.

A **right-branching structure** has the form:

$$\text{——————}\Big[\cdots\big[\cdots[\cdots\cdots]\big]\Big]$$

Ex: I called up the man who wrote the book that you told me about. (Chomsky, 1965:79/112-113)

C

C

(a) In a *phonological rule* **C** means: one and only one consonant. **C₀** (read C sub zero) stands for a string of zero or more consonants. **C₁** means at least one consonant.

The notion of consonant represented by C is any segment which is [+cons] or [−voc]. Therefore glides count as consonants.

(b) In syntax, **C** stands for concord in the *rewriting rule:*

$$C \to \begin{cases} \text{s in the context NP}_{\text{sing}} \text{—} \\ \phi \text{ in the context NP}_{\text{pl}} \text{—} \\ \text{past} \end{cases}$$

(Chomsky, 1957:39)

(c) Finally **C** also stands for "a collection of specified *syntactic features* (a *complex symbol*)." (Chomsky, 1965:84)

CATEGORIAL COMPONENT

In *Aspects*, Chomsky describes the **categorial component** as "the system of *rewriting rules* (which) carry out two separate functions: (1) they define the system of *grammatical relations*; (2) they determine the ordering of elements in *deep structures*." (Chomsky 1965:123)

S→ NP VP
VP→ V NP

In "Remarks on Nominalization," Chomsky develops a somewhat different view of the grammar, and he shows that "certain descriptive problems can be handled by enriching the lexicon and simplifying the categorial component of the *base* or conversely . . . the proper balance between various components of the grammar is entirely an empirical issue." (Chomsky, 1970a:13)

CATEGORIES

According to the *structuralist* syntactic theories, a grammar was regarded "as a system of classes of elements derived by analytic procedures of segmentation and classification." (Chomsky, 1970a:48)

Within the framework of the *Standard Theory*, "**categories** determine the abstract underlying form of each *formative*, the

syntactic function it can fulfil, and its semantic properties."
(Chomsky and Halle, 1968:7)

(a) **Grammatical categories** are composed of grammatical items
such as: Det(determiner), Aux(auxiliary), M(modal), Past, NP,
VP, etc. "The formative *inn* belongs to the syntactic categories
'noun', 'common', 'non-animate', 'count', etc." (Chomsky and
Halle, 1968:164)

(b) **Lexical categories** appear on the left in a lexical rule:

> M→ may
> N→ boy
> V→ frighten

M, N, V are lexical categories. "A lexical category or a category
that dominates a string ... X ... where X is a lexical category,
we shall call a major category ... All categories except Det (and
possibly M and Aux) are major categories." (Chomsky,
1965:74)

(c) **Phonological categories** are more generally called *features* in
the phonological matrix. "The formative *inn* belongs ... to the
phonological categories 'initial-vocalic', 'initial-nontense',
'second-consonantal', 'second-nasal' etc." (Chomsky and Halle,
1968:164)

(d) **Semantic categories** are not yet so well defined and are
supposed to specify the meaning of the formative. (*Ibid.*)

A *string* is categorized when it is subdivided into substrings, each of which is assigned to a certain category.

In "Remarks on Nominalization," where Chomsky develops the *lexicalist hypothesis,* he proposes to "eliminate the
distinction of feature and category, and regard all symbols of
the grammar as sets of features ... the reanalysis of phrase
categories as features permits the formulation of such base rules
as: Article → [± def, (NP)]." (Chomsky, 1970a:49)

(e) A **cyclic category** is a *node* that dominates the *transformational cycle,* i.e., the domain on which a transformation may
apply. $\bar{S}$ or $\bar{N}$ are cyclic categories. (See "Cycle, transformational.")

CLUSTERS

"In phonology a **weak cluster** is a string consisting of a simple *vocalic nucleus* (a simple vowel) followed by no more than one consonant"; examples: p*i*t, p*a*t, p*e*t, am*er-ic*-a.

"A **strong cluster** is a string consisting of either a simple vocalic nucleus followed by two or more consonants or a complex vocalic nucleus (a diphthong) followed by any number of consonants." examples: f*a*d*e*, w*isc-ons*-in, b*e*nd . . . (Chomsky and Halle, 1968: 29)

COGNITIVE CAPACITY

Cognitive capacity is an innate faculty of mind ("which is represented in some still-unknown way in the brain") to construct cognitive structures "that express systems of (unconscious) knowledge, belief, expectation, evaluation, judgment, and the like." (Chomsky, 1975c:21-24)

The **cognitive structure** is what is learned and, among its properties, the cognitive structure has the properties of universal grammar. (*Ibid*:29) Chomsky believes that the concept of cognitive structure is more appropriate than the notion of disposition or capacity which is "an unfortunate residue of empiricism." (*Ibid*.:23)

COGNIZE

Chomsky draws a distinction between the way a native speaker knows his language and the way a speaker knows a foreign language he has learned. In the first case, Chomsky suggests the verb **cognize** which includes the innate capacity of human beings for speaking, the principles of universal grammar, and the principles and rules of the internalized grammar both conscious and unconscious. (To cognize is closely linked to the notion of *competence*.) He then attributes to the verb **to know** a more restricted meaning which is the conscious "knowledge of" or "to know how" or a "scattered and chaotic subpart of the coherent and important systems and structures that are cognized." (Chomsky, 1975c: 165)

COMMAND

The notion of **command** is often used in the literature and has been defined by Langacker (1969): "We will say that a node A 'commands' another node B if (1) neither A nor B *dominates* the other; and (2) the S-node that most immediately dominates A also dominates B." (Quoted in Jackendoff, 1972)

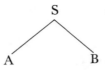

In the case of *Raising*, we have asymmetric command: NP commands S_2 but S_2 does not command NP.

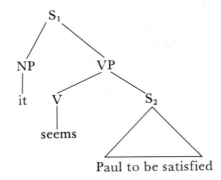

COMPETENCE

"Linguistic theory is concerned primarily with an ideal speaker-listener, in a completely homogeneous speech-community, who knows its language perfectly and is unaffected by such grammatically irrelevant conditions as memory limitations, distractions, shifts of attention and interest, and errors." (Chomsky, 1965:3)

"**Competence** refers to the ability of the idealized speaker-hearer to associate sounds and meanings strictly in accordance with the rules of his language." (Chomsky, 1972a:116)

Competence is the knowledge of a language the speaker has acquired, "the system of rules he has internalized and that determines relationship between sound and meaning for indefinitely many sentences. Of course the person who knows a language perfectly has little or no conscious knowledge of the rules that he uses constantly in speaking or hearing, writing or reading, or internal monologue." (Chomsky and Halle, 1968:3)

A *generative grammar* can be regarded only "as a characterization of the intrinsic tacit knowledge or competence that underlies actual *performance*."(Chomsky, 1965:140)

COMPLEMENT SENTENCE

A **complement sentence** is an *embedded* sentence introduced by a *COMP node* in the *deep structure* and by a *complementizer* (which can be deleted) in the *surface structure*. The sentence "I believe that John saw Bill" has the following underlying structure:

When the complement sentence is dominated by the NP object as in the case of sentences with verbs of the same group as *believe*, the embedded sentence is also called a **sentential object**. If the complement sentence is dominated by the NP subject, the embedded sentence is called a **sentential subject** as in "That John saw Bill worries me."

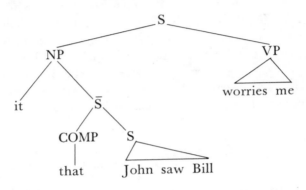

A COMP node can introduce other sentences than complement sentences; in *Conditions on Transformations* (Chomsky 1973), all sentences come from: $\bar{S} \rightarrow$ COMP-S.

COMPLEMENTARY DISTRIBUTION
According to the traditional terminology, in phonology, two elements which have no contexts in common are said to be in **complementary distribution.**

COMPLEMENTIZER (COMP)
A **complementizer** is a particle which is placed in the initial position of a *complement sentence*. *That, for-to, poss-ing* (or *'s-ing*) are the complementizers dominated by the COMP *node* in:

> *That* Mary sings pleases me.
> *For* Mary *to* sing is a pleasure.
> I enjoy Mary*'s* sing*ing*.

Chomsky suggests that +WH is the COMP underlying direct or indirect questions and -WH is the COMP underlying relative clauses. Whether the complementizer is introduced into an embedded sentence by a *phrase-structure rule* S̄→COMP - S (Chomsky 1970a, 1973 and Bresnan 1972) or transformationally (Rosenbaum 1967), transformational linguists agree that *WH-movement* is a *transformation* which applies after the complementizer has been introduced. It is a *cyclic* rule.

COMPLEMENTIZER SUBSTITUTION

Complementizer Substitution Universal is a principle which states that "only languages with clause-initial *COMP* permit a COMP substitution transformation. This principle presupposes that COMP is a universal element that may appear in different sentence positions and asserts that an item can be moved in a COMP position only when COMP is initial." (Chomsky, 1973:234)

Ex: I-expect- [[COMP]John will leave] → I expect *that* John will leave I-expect [[COMP]John to leave] → I expect John to leave

COMPLEX SYMBOL (CS)

A **complex symbol** is a collection of *features* which characterize a lexical entry. "For ease of exposition, we shall regard a lexical entry as a matrix-complex symbol pair (D, C) . . . where D is a phonological distinctive feature matrix 'spelling' a certain lexical *formative* and C is a collection of specified *syntactic features*." (Chomsky, 1965:84)

"For example, the *formative* 'inn' belongs to the *syntactic categories* 'noun', 'common', 'non-animate', 'count', etc.; to certain *semantic categories* which specify its meaning; and to the *phonological categories* 'initial-vocalic', 'initial-nontense', 'second-consonantal', 'second-nasal', etc. The lexical entry 'inn' is simply the complex of these categories, and the terminal symbol 'inn' ... is nothing other than the complex symbol consisting of this set of category specifications." (Chomsky and Halle, 1968:164)

In other words, a formative is called a complex symbol because it is a collection of phonological, syntactic and semantic properties.

CONCATENATION

Concatenation is used to indicate that the elements of a sentence are chained together in a particular order. Usually the plus-sign is used to symbolize the link. "Thus on the morphemic level in English we have the vocabulary elements *the, boy, S, past, come*, etc., and we can form the string the+boy+S+come+past, representing the utterance 'the boys came'." (Chomsky, 1957:109)

CONDITIONS AND CONSTRAINTS

"Knowledge of a language can be expressed in the form of a system of *rules* (*a grammar*) that generates the language. To approach the fundamental empirical problem, we attempt to restrict the class of potential human languages by setting various **conditions** on the form and function of grammars; the term '*universal grammar*' has commonly been used to refer to the system of general **constraints** of this sort ... There are (1) conditions on the systems that qualify as grammars, (2) conditions on the way the rules of a grammar apply to generate *structural descriptions*." (Chomsky, 1973:1)

CONSTITUENT

A **constituent** is any phrase of a sentence belonging to a *syntactic category*, NP, VP, N, V etc. "It is the 'significant occurrence' of a *string* X in a containing string Z. Thus 'called up' is a constituent of 'I called up my friends' but not of 'I called up the stairs.'" (Chomsky, 1975d:69)

CO-OCCURRENCE

The method of analysis of the morphological structure, based on **co-occurrence**, was introduced by Harris in order to discover the possible environment of *morphemes* that occur in a sentence. Chomsky rejects the co-occurrence method of analysis, as used by the distributionalists, on the grounds that it is "a relation defined on actual sentences," or in other words, at the level of *surface structure*. (Chomsky, 1964b:83 and 1974a)

CREATIVITY

In the Chomskyan terminology, **creativity** is a consequence of generativity; creativity belongs to the domain of *performance*, while generativity—the recursive property of grammars—belongs to the domain of *competence*. "The creative aspect of language use' refers to a property of the use of language . . . It is innovative, unbounded in scope, free from the control of external stimuli or detectable physiological states, coherent and appropriate to situations, engendering in the listener thoughts related to those of the speaker . . . The recursive property of generative grammars provides the means for the creative aspect of language use." (Chomsky, 1974b:28)

CYCLE

The notion of **transformational cycle** has been developed by Chomsky in *Aspects* (1965:29, 35-36). It means that *transformational rules*, phonological or syntactic, apply in a recursive manner to successive constituents (to which the rule is applicable) starting from the most deeply *embedded* and going to the most dominant constituent (or clause). It is a *formal linguistic universal*.

Given the following string: [N[A ortho[S doks]S]A]y]N, in the first cycle the transformational rule of stress applies to the smallest *constituent* [doks]. When the *brackets* are erased and the rules can apply to the next largest constituent [orthodoks], it is the second cycle. The second pairs of brackets are erased and the third and last cycle is reached [orthodoksy]. It is the *maximal domain*. (Chomsky and Halle, 1968: 133)

   WH-movement is a cyclic rule:
(a) COMP they believed [COMP Mary said [COMP John saw someone.]] On the innermost cycle wh-movement applies to (a) to give:
(b) COMP they believed [COMP Mary said [that John saw someone.]] On the second cycle we derive (c) by wh-movement again:
(c) COMP they believed [that Mary said that John saw someone.] On the last cycle we derive (d) by wh-movement and the obligatory rules of auxiliary inversion and case assignment:
(d) Who did they believe that Mary said that John saw? The application of cyclic rules is constrained by the "Strict Cycle Condition" which says: "No rule can apply to a domain *dominated* by a cyclic *node* A in such a way as to affect solely a proper subdomain of A *dominated* by a *node* B which is also a cyclic node. In other words, rules cannot return to earlier stages of the cycle after the *derivation* has moved to larger, more inclusive domains." (Chomsky, 1973:243)

D

DATA

Linguistic **data** are a collection of utterances selected from a corpus.

   "The **primary linguistic data** consist of signals classified as sentences and nonsentences, and a partial and tentative pairing of signals with *structural descriptions*" (Chomsky, 1965:32)

In a hypothetical language acquisition device, the primary linguistic data constitute the "input."

The **formal linguistic data** are the phonological representation of the data. They imply a semantic notion.

DEEP STRUCTURE

The term **deep structure** is used to refer to the abstract mental representation which underlies an utterance. Chomsky claims that the notion of *deep structure* and *surface structure* can be traced to the *Port-Royal* Grammar: "According to the Port-Royal theory, surface structure corresponds only to sound—to the corporeal aspect of language; but when the signal is produced, with its surface structure, there takes place a corresponding mental analysis into what we may call the deep structure, a formal structure that relates directly not to the sound but to the meaning." (Chomsky, 1972 a: 16)

The type of information carried in the deep structure has changed over time. "In the *standard theory*, deep structures were characterized in terms of two properties: their role in syntax initiating transformational derivations, and their role in semantic interpretation. As for the latter, it was postulated that deep structures give all the information required for determining the meaning of sentences." (Chomsky, 1975c:81) In the *extended standard theory*, the concept of deep structure is narrowed and semantic interpretation applies to surface structures only. Finally, in *Reflections on Language*, Chomsky discards the term *deep structure* which he considers misleading and prefers "initial phrase marker" as being more appropriate.

DELETION

Deletion is considered as an elementary *transformation* and Chomsky explains how it applies: "A transformation can delete an element only if this element is the designated representative of a *category*, or if the *structural condition* that defines this transformation states that the deleted element is structurally identical to another element of the transformed *string*." (Chomsky, 1964b: 71)

Agent-deletion or *it-deletion* can illustrate the first point, *Equi-NP-deletion* illustrates the second. Deletion is sometimes called erasure.

DERIVATION

A **derivation** is "a finite sequence of *strings,* beginning with an initial string of Σ" (Σ=#sentence#) and such that "each string in the sequence is derived from the preceding string by application of one of the instruction formulas of F" (F=set of instruction formulas). (Chomsky 1957:29)

Given the following set of instruction formulas or rules:

S→NP VP   (read: rewrite S as NP and VP)
VP→V NP (" :   " VP " V " NP)
NP→Det N (" :   " NP " Det and N)
V→hit   (" :   " V " hit)
Det→the   (" :   " Det " the)
N→man, ball(" :   " N " man, ball)

If we apply one single rule to one element only on each line, we obtain the following sequence of strings of symbols which is called a derivation:

S
NP VP
NP V NP
Det N V NP
Det N V Det N
Det N hit Det N
the N hit the N
the man hit the ball

The last line is the *terminal string*. It cannot be rewritten any further.

A **sequential derivation** is a derivation in which the rules used to produce each line of the derivation apply only once and in some given order. (Chomsky, 1965:67)

DERIVATIONAL CONSTRAINT

This term used by Lakoff can be replaced by its equivalent "rule of grammar."

(See discussion in Chomsky, 1972b:140-141.)

DERIVED CONSTITUENT STRUCTURE

A **derived constituent structure** is the structure which results from a *derived phrase-marker*. (Chomsky, 1961a:135) (See "phrase-marker.")

The sentence "Turn out some of the lights" has the following phrase-marker:

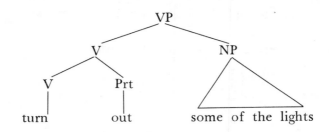

If the *particle-movement transformation* applies, it will give a new P-marker called derived P-marker, and the new structure will be a derived constituent structure.

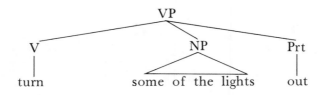

DERIVED SENTENCE

"A sentence of the language formed by applying certain optional *transformations*, as well as all obligatory rules, of course, will be called a **derived sentence**." (Chomsky, 1962: 223)

Thus, if passive transformation is applied to the string:

John - past - see - Bill

it will generate the derived sentence:

Bill was seen by John.

DETERMINER (Det)

In a *structural description*, **Det** is the modifier of a noun. It can be an article, a pronoun, or a quantifier.

Within the *lexicalist theory*, it is proposed that determiners are generated by the following phrase-structure rules:

$$\text{Det} \rightarrow (\text{Prearticle } of) \text{ Article (Postarticle)}$$
$$\text{Article} \rightarrow \left\{ \begin{matrix} \pm \text{ def} \\ \text{Poss} \end{matrix} \right\}$$

Under this analysis, the phrase "several of John's" in the string "several of John's proofs of the theorem" would have the structure:

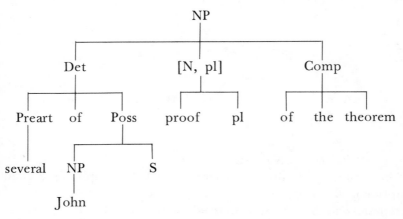

(Chomsky 1970a:36-37)

DEVIANCE/DEVIATION

Deviance or **deviation** takes place when the constraints imposed by the *selectional rules* are relaxed. There can be various degrees of deviation as exemplified by the following sentences: "Sincerity may virtue the boy/sincerity may elapse the boy/ sincerity may admire the boy." (Chomsky, 1965:152-153)

DISCOURSE

In structural linguistics, the meaning of the word **discourse** has been widely debated. "Discourse is either considered as speech (the Saussurean *parole*), or as a manifestation of language (in Hjelmslevean sense)." (Parret, *Language and Discourse*:245)

Chomsky does not recognize that dichotomy. "Actual discourse consists, by definition, of utterances . . . we might consider ideal discourse that consists of sentences, abstracting away from the factors that interact with grammar in performance . . . In such an ideal discourse, certain elements are interpreted by principles that extend beyond the sentence, certain anaphoric processes being the clearest example. Of course, in actual discourse, interpretation involves factors that go beyond the discourse: e.g., presupposed common beliefs, situational context, etc." (Chomsky, 1974b:39)

"The domain of discourse must be related to the categories of common-sense understanding, though how closely is a fair question." (Chomsky, 1975c:45)

DOMINATE

In a *tree diagram*, all the elements which are under the same *node* form one *constituent*. The constituent whose label is directly above one or several connected nodes is said to **dominate** the other constituents. In the diagram, S dominates NP_1 and VP, NP_1 dominates Det and N, etc.

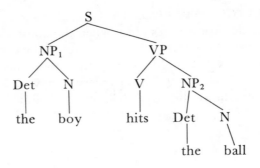

(See "Command.")

DUMMY ELEMENT

In a *phrase-marker*, a **dummy element** Δ is an abstract element representing any *category*. Later on, in the *transformation*, it is obligatorily replaced. (Chomsky, 1966a:64)

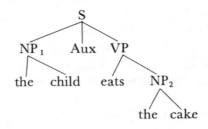

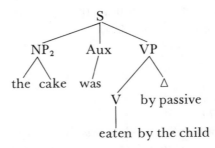

"The passive transformation substitutes NP₁ for the dummy element passive and places NP₂ in the position of

NP$_1$." (Chomsky, 1965:104) The passive transformation has been a much debated issue. See the Appendix for another approach.

E

EMBEDDING/NESTING

Embedding (sometimes also called *nesting*) is a simple case of subordination. Example:

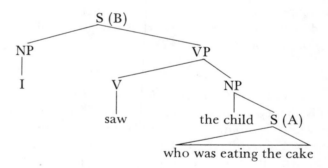

"The phrases A and B form a nested [or embedded] construction if A falls totally within B, with some nonnull element to its left within B and some nonnull element to its right within B." (Chomsky, 1965:12)

Self-embedding is a particular case of embedding. "The phrase A is self-embedded in B if A is nested in B and, furthermore, A is a phrase of the same type as B. Thus, in the sentence 'The man who the boy who the students recognized pointed out is a friend of mine.' 'who the students recognized' is self-embedded in 'who the boy . . . . pointed out', since both clauses are relative." (Chomsky, 1965:12)

ERASURE
(See "Deletion.")

ESSENTIAL PROPERTY
In the Aristotelian logic, an **essential property** is an attribute common and peculiar to all members of a species. In a discussion about the nature of cognitive capacity, Chomsky mentions "the notion 'essential properties', referring it to the systems of language and common-sense understanding." (Chomsky, 1975c:46)

EVALUATION (See "Generalization.")
"The major problem in constructing an **evaluation** measure for grammars is that of determining which *generalizations* about a language are significant ones; . . . choice of an evaluation measure constitutes a decision as to what are 'similar processes' and 'natural classes'—in short, what are significant generalizations." (Chomsky, 1965:42)

EXTENDED STANDARD THEORY
This theory proposes some revisions in order to solve certain inadequacies found in the standard theory, essentially as regards *semantic interpretation*. The **Extended Standard Theory** claims that semantic representation is determined jointly by the *deep structure* and *surface structure*.

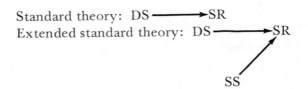

This new theory narrows the content of the deep structure and increases the descriptive power of the surface structure:

(1) deep structure determines grammatical relations;

(2) surface structure determines some aspects of semantic interpretation such as focus and presupposition;

(3) deep and surface structure determine other aspects of
semantic interpretation such as coreference. (Chomsky,
1972:134)

In *Reflections on Language*, Chomsky further reduces the
content of the *initial phrase marker* (formerly called *deep
structure*) and increases the role of the *surface structure*: "I will
further suggest that perhaps all semantic information is determined by a somewhat enriched notion of surface structure . . .
We can tentatively postulate that only surface structures under-
go semantic interpretation." (Chomsky, 1975c:116)

F

FACTORIZATION

A *string* is **factored** (or *analyzed*) when its elements are
separated into *constituents*. A string is properly factored when
each of its factors matches the factors of the *structural description* (SD) of a given *transformational rule*. Each factor can be
followed by one variable, and it is the constant *categories* which
change, not the *variables*. (See "Analyzability.")

FEATURES, DIACRITIC

Diacritic features are used, in lexical entries, to represent a
peripheral classification, for instance declensional classes which

have no syntactic function. The diacritic features have two sources, the *lexicon* and the *readjustment rules*. (Chomsky and Halle, 1968:373-376)

FEATURES, DISTINCTIVE

Distinctive features are the minimal elements of which phonetic, lexical and phonological transcriptions are composed by combination and *concatenation*. Distinctive features have two functions: (a) classificatory, (b) phonetic.

"As **classificatory** devices, the distinctive features play a role in the full specification of a lexical entry." In their classificatory function all features are binary: [± round], [± back] [± nasal], etc. (Chomsky and Halle, 1968:65)

"In their phonetic function, features receive a physical interpretation . . . They provide a representation of an utterance which can be interpreted as a set of instructions to the physical articulatory system, or as a refined level of perceptual representation." (Chomsky and Halle, 1968:65)

"In their phonetic function, [**phonetic features**] are scales that admit a fixed number of values, and they relate independently controllable aspects of the speech event or independent elements of perceptual representation." (Chomsky and Halle, 1968:298) For example, /i/ "is to be understood as an abbreviation for a feature complex or a unit such as:

$$
\begin{bmatrix}
+\text{segment} \\
+\text{vocalic} \\
-\text{consonantal} \\
+\text{high} \\
-\text{low} \\
-\text{back} \\
-\text{round} \\
-\text{tense}
\end{bmatrix} \text{"} \qquad \text{(Chomsky and Halle, 1968:64)}
$$

The **prosodic features** are another class of phonetic features. The term refers essentially to the stress and tone of utterances. "Prosodic features are features whose domain extends over sequences that are longer than a word." (Chomsky and Halle, 1968:68)

FEATURES, LEXICAL

A **lexical feature** of a stem or noun is a prefix which is generally assigned no category at all but might be regarded syntactically on a par with other *inherent features* of a lexical entry. "The underlying representation of *monogenesis* identifies *genesis* as a noun which is an independent word and assigns *mono-* to no category." (Chomsky and Halle, 1968:100)

Paul Postal has suggested that in such cases the prefix might be considered as a lexical feature of the stem or noun. (*Ibid.*, footnote 51)

FILTER

A **filter** is a constraint which marks sentences as ungrammatical.

"The *transformational rules* act as a 'filter' that permits only certain *generalized Phrase-markers* to qualify as *deep structures*." (Chomsky, 1965:139)

Perlmutter claims that filters can also be *surface structure* constraints. (Perlmutter, 1971:19)

Finally, Chomsky admits: "It remains an open question whether rules of interpretation and filters must also apply to what have been called 'shallow structures'." (Chomsky, 1973:284, note 69)

In any case, transformational rules have a filtering function and prevent any inadequate operation from applying.

FINITE-STATE GRAMMAR

A **finite-state** language is an artificial language produced by a machine which runs through a sequence of states and produces a word with each transition; each transition and each production corresponds to an instruction or grammatical rule. The machine has an initial state and a final state. Such a machine is called a **finite-state grammar**. Each state represents the grammatical restrictions that limit the choice of the next word at this point of the utterance. (Chomsky, 1957:19)

No natural language can be characterized by such a machine because human languages are non-finite, e.g., they can produce infinitely many sentences. (Chomsky, 1957:23-25)

FOCUS AND PRESUPPOSITION

"The **focus** and **presupposition** designate what information in the sentence is intended to be new and what is intended to be old." (Jackendoff, 1972:3)

Chomsky wonders if these notions can be characterized in grammatical terms and if they can be determined from the *deep structure* or in terms of *surface structure*. "The notions 'focus', 'presupposition', and 'shared presupposition' (even in cases where the presupposition may not be expressible by a grammatical sentence) must be determinable from the *semantic interpretation* of sentences if we are to be able to explain how discourse is constructed and, in general, how language is used." (Chomsky, 1972b:89-100)

"One speaks of the presupposition of a sentence, within semantic theory, as what must be true for the sentence to have a truth value . . . In another sense, one speaks of the presupposition of the speaker, that is, what he intends the hearer to assume as true when he uses an *utterance* in one of the permissible ways." (Chomsky, 1974b:46)

FORMAL THEORY

"In the strict sense of the word, an argument, a characterization, a theory, etc., is **formal** if it deals with form as opposed to meaning, that is, if it deals solely with the shape and arrangement of symbols." (Chomsky, 1975d:83)

"A **formalized** theory is one that is formulated in accordance with certain clear canons of rigor and precision." (*Ibid.*)

(See discussion of formal universals in "Universals.")

FORMATIVES

Formatives are the elements which appear on the last line of a *derivation*, that is to say, after all the rules have applied. There are lexical formatives (*boy, sincerity*), grammatical formatives (past, ic, ion, #) and formative strings (tele+graph+ic). Formatives are more traditionally called *morphemes*. (Chomsky and Halle, 1968:9)

G

GENERALIZATION

The aim of a grammar is to capture the linguistically significant **generalizations** about a language and express them by *rules*, conditions and notation. "We have a generalization when a set of rules about distinct items can be replaced by a single rule (or, more generally, partially identical rules) about the whole set, or when it can be shown that a 'natural class' of items undergoes a certain process or set of similar processes." (Chomsky, 1965:42)

For instance, in phonology, the following rules apply in French:

$$a \longrightarrow \tilde{a}$$
$$o \longrightarrow \tilde{o}$$
$$\varepsilon \longrightarrow \tilde{\varepsilon}$$
$$\ddot{u} \longrightarrow \tilde{œ}$$

when the vowel is followed by a nasal consonant which is itself either at the end of a word or followed by a consonant. These rules can be generalized and expressed:

$$V \longrightarrow \tilde{V} \; / \; \underline{\hspace{1cm}} \; N \begin{Bmatrix} \# \\ C \end{Bmatrix}$$

[Read: a vowel (V) becomes a nasal vowel ($\tilde{V}$) in the context (/) where it is followed (−) by a nasal consonant (N) which is followed either by nothing (#) or by a consonant (C).]

Another example will illustrate generalization in syntax:

$$\bar{X} \rightarrow X \ldots \text{(where X can be any one of N, A, or V)}$$
$$\text{(Chomsky, 1970a:52)}$$

GENERALIZED TRANSFORMATION
(See "Transformation.")

GENERATIVE CAPACITY
A grammar has both a weak and a strong generative capacity. Its **weak generative capacity** refers to the set of *strings* that it can generate, while its **strong generative capacity** refers to the set of *structural descriptions* that it can generate. "The study of strong generative capacity is related to the study of *descriptive adequacy* . . . The study of weak generative capacity is of rather marginal linguistic interest." (Chomsky, 1965:60)

GENERATIVE GRAMMAR
A **generative grammar** is a grammar able to describe a language and establish rules which account for the potential utterances of that particular language. The three major components of a generative grammar are: the *syntactic, phonological* and *semantic components*. (Chomsky, 1957:48; 1965:16)

A sentence is **generated** by a *grammar* when all the rules enumerated in the corresponding *derivation* have applied. (Chomsky, 1957:46-48)

Chomsky indicates that there are two conflicting models of generative grammar: (1) the *taxonomic model* and (2) the *transformational* model. "In the case of the taxonomic model, the syntactic component consists of an unordered set of *rewriting rules* . . . The phonological component consists of two distinct sets of (unordered) rewriting rules, . . . (a) the *morpho-phonemic* rules and (b) the *phonetic* rules . . . The transformational model is far more complex and highly structured. The syntactic component is assumed to consist of two sub-components. The first (*constituent structure*) subcomponent consists of an ordered set of rewriting rules that generate strings of formatives . . . The second (transformational) subcomponent consists of a partially ordered set of complex operations called (*grammatical*) *transformations* . . . The phonological component . . . consists of an ordered set of rewriting rules, an ordered set of transformational rules, and an ordered set of rewriting rules, in that order. The transformational rules apply in a *cycle.*" (Chomsky, 1964b:52-54)

GENERATIVE SEMANTICS

Generative Semantics is the theory developed by Lakoff, Postal, Ross and others. It is a semantically-based grammar. The main originality of this theory is related to the *semantic representation*: "Semantic representation = $(P_1, PR, Top, F, \ldots)$, where PR is a conjunction of presuppositions, Top is an indication of the 'topic' of the sentence, F is the indication of the focus, and . . . indicates other elements of semantic representation that might be needed." (Lakoff, 1969b) quoted by Chomsky, (1972:135).

For Chomsky's criticism of this theory, see Chomsky, 1972:134-136, 139-142.

GLOBAL RULES

The term **global rules**, as used by Lakoff, has the same meaning as *derivational constraints*. It refers to "rules that apply, not to the last *phrase marker* of a *derivation* so far constructed, but to a set of phrase markers already derived." (Chomsky, 1975c:117)

Chomsky refers to these rules and rejects them on the grounds that they increase the class of admissible grammars. (See discussion in Chomsky 1972b: 139-141 and 1975c: 117-118.)

GRAMMAR

In modern linguistics **"grammar"** has a broader meaning than in the traditional usage.

"We use the term 'grammar' with a systematic ambiguity. On the one hand, the term refers to the explicit theory constructed by the linguist and proposed as a description of the speaker's *competence*. On the other hand, we use the term to refer to this competence itself. The former usage is familiar; the latter, though perhaps less familiar, is equally appropriate." (Chomsky and Halle, 1968:3)

It means the speaker's knowledge of a language which includes sound, meaning and syntax.

More technically, it also means "a device that *generates* all the grammatical sequences of (a language) L and none of the ungrammatical ones." It can then be considered as a "tripartite structure" with: (1) "a sequence of rules from which phrase structure can be reconstructed, (2) a sequence of *morphophonemic rules* that convert strings of morphemes into strings of phonemes and, connecting these sequences, (3) a sequence of *transformational rules* that carry strings with phrase structure into new strings to which the morphophonemic rules can apply." (Chomsky, 1957:13, 107)

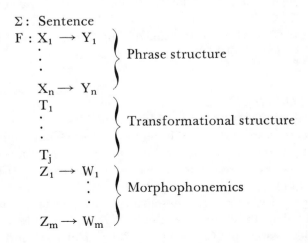

"A grammar is called **context-free** (or simple) if in each rule of the form A → Z/X — Y, X and Y are null, so that the rules apply independent of context. In a **context-sensitive** grammar X and Y are not null and impose a number of restrictions in a rule of the form A → Z/X—Y."(Chomsky, 1965: 67, 92)

Example of a context-free rule:

S → NP VP

Example of a context-sensitive rule:

V → [+ V, + Transitive] / — NP

(Read: a verb is a transitive verb when it is followed by a noun-phrase.)

GRAMMATICAL/GRAMMATICALNESS

Chomsky uses the terms **grammatical** or degree of **grammaticalness** in a specific nonprescriptive sense, that is to say, he does not imply any censorship. He shows that the study of semi-grammatical utterances may significantly illuminate the notions of grammar. The degree of grammaticalness is a measure which indicates in what respect an utterance is deviant. (Chomsky, 1961:235-237)

In the *Extended Standard Theory*, various devices are explored to determine grammaticalness: "rules of the *categorial component* of the *base*, lexical *transformations* involving contextual features, nonlexical transformations of various sorts, surface *filters*, rules of interpretations involving *deep* and *surface structures*. Only if a *derivation* satisfies all of these conditions does its final *terminal string* qualify as a grammatical sentence." (Chomsky, 1973:284)

GRAMMATICAL RELATIONS

Grammatical relations indicate how words are connected in a sentence. For instance, in "Sincerity may frighten the boy" the grammatical relation between *sincerity* and *frighten* is Subject-Verb and between *frighten* and *the boy*, Verb-Object. "Such relations can be defined derivatively in terms of the functional notions suggested earlier. Thus Subject-Verb can be defined as the relation between the Subject-of a Sentence and Main-Verb-of the Predicate-of the Sentence, . . . and Verb-Object can be defined as the relation between the Main-Verb-of and the Direct-Object-of a *VP*.

"The semantically significant functional notions (grammatical relations) are directly represented in *base structures*, and only in these . . . " (Chomsky, 1965:73/117)

In a tree representation the *subject* of a sentence is the NP directly *dominated* by S; the object of a verb is the NP directly dominated by VP.

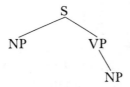

GRAMMATICAL TRANSFORMATION

Grammatical transformation is a notion introduced by Harris, and it is defined "as a (symmetrical) relation holding between two sentence forms if corresponding positions in the two forms are filled by the same n-tuples of expressions. This relation is not part of *generative grammar* . . . it is a structural relation holding of sentences and sentence forms described by a *taxonomic, IC grammar*." (Chomsky, 1964b:83)

Chomsky also uses the term *grammatical transformation* in the sense of *generative transformation*, that is to say, a series of operations which apply on abstract structures and generate well-formed sentences. "A grammatical transformation is a

mapping of *P-markers* into P-markers. (sic)" (Chomsky, 1964b:131)
   (See *"Transformations."*)

H

HOMONYMY

"When the simplest grammar provides nonequivalent *derivations* for some sentence, we say that we have a case of **constructional homonymity,** and we can suggest this formal property as an explanation for the *semantic ambiguity* of the sentence in question. The sentence 'they are flying planes' is a case in point and can be assigned two phrase structures: 'they-are-flying planes' or 'they-are flying-planes.' "

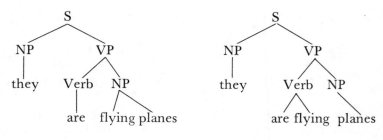

(Chomsky, 1956:114)

HOUSEKEEPING RULES

Housekeeping rules refer to minor *transformations* which consist in adjustments, such as agreement, and come after major transformations have applied. The term was introduced by Emmon Bach. (See "Questions" for *Linguistic Inquiry*, Spring 1971.)

I

IMMEDIATE CONSTITUTENTS

The analysis in **immediate constituents** was first practiced by Bloomfield and was subsequently elaborated by Rulon S. Wells. It is an account of *surface structure*; Chomsky calls it also *labeled bracketing*. The immediate constituents are *formatives,* or sequences of formatives. The following diagram retains just what is essential for the determination of the phrase structure (constituent analysis) of the derived sentence "The man hit the ball".

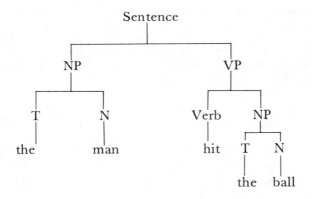

"A sequence of words of this sentence is a constituent of type Z if we can trace this sequence back to a single point of origin in the diagram, and this point of origin is labelled Z. Thus 'hit the ball' can be traced to VP; hence 'hit the ball' is a VP in the derived sentence. But 'man hit' cannot be traced back to any single point of origin in the diagram; hence 'man hit' is not a constituent at all." (Chomsky, 1957:27-28)

(See Rulon S. Wells: "Immediate Constituents" in *Language,* 23:81-117, 1947.)

INNATENESS
Chomsky's philosophy is in direct opposition to behaviorism. In answer to the framework of stimulus-response psychology, he postulates that the mind possesses an **innate** schema of *universal grammar* which makes possible language learning.

"A child who has learned a language has developed an internal representation of a system of rules that determine how sentences are to be formed, used, and understood ... As a long-range task for general linguistics, we might set the problem of developing an account of this innate linguistic theory that provides the basis for language learning." (Chomsky, 1965:25)

INTERPRETIVE COMPONENTS
The two **interpretive components** of a *generative grammar* are the *phonological component* and the *semantic component*. (Chomsky, 1964b:52)

INTUITION
According to Chomsky, **intuition** is only one of the devices used in the discovery procedure: "One may arrive at a grammar by intuition, guess-work, all sorts of partial methodological hints, reliance on past experience, etc." (Chomsky, 1957:56). Yet intuition is essential: "It is important to bear in mind that when an operational procedure is proposed, it must be tested for *adequacy* (exactly as a theory of linguistic intuition—a *grammar*—must be tested for adequacy) by measuring it against the standard provided by the tacit knowledge that it attempts to specify and describe." (Chomsky, 1965:19)

INVARIANCE
A formative or a segment of a formative meets the condition of **invariance** when its *phonological representation* is in no way altered on account of its context.

"We may say that a *formative* meets the condition of **invariance** when the *phonological matrix* given in its lexical entry is a submatrix of the *phonetic matrix* corresponding to it in each context in which it occurs. Thus the formative *inn* meets the invariance condition, but the formative *algebra* does not. The lexical entry for *algebra* must specify that the final vowel is nontense; otherwise, it will not be stressless, nor will it reduce to [ə]." (Chomsky and Halle, 1968:166)

J

JUNCTURAL ELEMENTS

Junctural elements are *word boundaries* and are introduced by *syntactic rules*. (Chomsky, 1964b:85)

(See "Boundary.")

K

KERNEL

"We define the **kernel** of the language as the set of sentences that are produced when we apply only obligatory *transformations* to the *terminal strings* of the *grammar*." (Chomsky 1957:45)

"One must be careful not to confuse kernel sentences with the *basic strings* that underlie them." (Chomsky, 1965:18) Example: "John washes John" is a basic string underlying the kernel sentence: "John washes himself."

L

LANGUE AND PAROLE

According to Ferdinand de Saussure, **langue** (language) is both a social product of the faculty of speech and a collection of necessary conventions that have been adopted by a social body to permit individuals to exercise that faculty. By opposition, **parole** (speaking) is an individual act. (Saussure, 1966:9-14)

In a discussion, Chomsky borrows the words *langue* and *parole* from Saussure. "The *generative grammar* internalized by someone who has acquired a language defines what in Saussurian terms we may call langue." But he later stresses the shortcomings contained in the notions: "Saussure, like Whitney, regards langue as basically a store of signs with their grammatical properties, that is, a store of word-like elements, fixed phrases and, perhaps, certain limited phrase types . . . He was thus quite unable to come to grips with the recursive processes underlying sentence formation, and he appears to regard sentence formation as a matter of parole rather than langue . . . " (Chomsky, 1964b:52-60)

LEXICAL REPRESENTATION

"We shall use the term **lexical representation** in reference to *formatives* which are provided directly by the *lexicon*, i.e., the lexical formatives as well as certain grammatical formatives which happen to appear in lexical entries." (Chomsky and Halle, 1968:9)

"The lexical representation for the word *telegraph* should be + tele+graef+, where each of the symbols t, e, . . . is to be understood as an informal abbreviation for a certain set of *phonological categories* (*distinctive feature*). Thus the lexical representation is abstract in a very clear sense; it relates to the signal only indirectly, through the medium of the rules of *phonological interpretation* that apply to it as determined by its intrinsic abstract representation and the *surface structures* in which it appears." (Chomsky and Halle, 1968:12)

LEXICALIST HYPOTHESIS

In his article on "Nominalizations," Chomsky presents two approaches to the analysis of the internal structure of the nominal phrase: the **lexicalist** and the **transformationalist positions**. According to the "lexicalist position," the *base rules* are extended and the *transformational component* simplified. According to the "transformationalist position," (Lakoff, 1965) the base structures are simplified and the transformational component extended. (Chomsky, 1970a:17-22)

LEXICON

"The **lexicon** is an unordered list of all lexical *formatives;* it is a set of lexical entries, each lexical entry being a pair (D, C) where D is a phonological *distinctive feature matrix* 'spelling' a certain lexical formative and C is a collection of specified *syntactic features*." (Chomsky, 1965:84)

Example: *eat* [+V, (+−NP)], *elapse* [+V +−#]

(Read: *eat* is a verb (+V) which may be followed by a direct object (+−NP), *elapse* is a verb (+V) which has no direct object (+−#).)

The lexicon is one of the two parts of the *base* system. "It is concerned with all properties, idiosyncratic or redundant, of individual lexical items." (Chomsky, 1972a:140-141)

LINGUISTIC DISPOSITION

Linguistic disposition is an innate capacity "to acquire a certain *competence* (i.e., a certain cognitive structure, a grammar, knowledge of language)." (Chomsky, 1975c:222)

LINGUISTIC LEVELS

Linguistic levels are constructed by the linguists as a device to divide the complexity of the description of a language. Each level is a specific set of *primes* and "presents a unidimensional point of view from which to investigate the structure of the grammatical utterances." The levels are organized in a hierarchy: the lowest level of description is the phonetic level, then the phonological level, the word level, the category level, the morphological level, the phrase-structure level; the highest level of description is the transformational level. Each of these levels has a proper internal structure. It is a concatenation algebra and each level can be *mapped* into other levels.

Each representation is the "spelling" in terms of elements of one linguistic level. (Chomsky, 1975d:Ch. 3)

LOGICAL FORM

The **logical form** is the expression of a sentence in a form involving *quantifiers* and other logical notions in such a way as to reveal its logical structure. The logical form of the sentence: "The police think who the FBI discovered that Bill shot" is: the police think for which person x, the FBI discovered that Bill shot x. (Chomsky, 1975c:93-94)

M

MAPPING

Mapping is represented by the symbol Φ and it consists in carrying over the elements of one *level of representation* into another level.

According to the *Standard Theory* (Chomsky, 1965) the *deep structure* is mapped into *semantic interpretation* while the *surface structure* is mapped into *phonetic representation*. In the *Extended Standard Theory* (Chomsky, 1970a), both the deep structure and the surface structure are mapped into semantic interpretation.

MARKEDNESS

Phonetic *segments* are specified by *phonetic features* (p[+stop] , [−voice] etc . . .). If a segment has the more likely specification (+ or −) for some feature, it is said to be **unmarked** for that feature; if not, it is said to be **marked**. For example, in every language there are voiceless stops; in some languages there are no voiced stops; therefore, it is more likely for a stop to be voiceless. Voiceless stops are said to be unmarked for the feature *voice* while voiced stops are said to be marked for that feature.

The notion of markedness has been developed into a theory within the framework of generative phonology, in chapter 9 of *The Sound Pattern of English*.

MATRIX

A **classificatory matrix** is a table in which the columns stand for *segments* and the rows for *categories*. (See "Phonetic Representation and "Phonological Matrix.")

A **matrix sentence** and a **matrix predicate** refer to a main sentence and a main predicate in opposition to an *embedded* sentence and an embedded predicate. "The terms 'matrix sentence' and 'constituent sentence' are due to Lees (*The Grammar of English Nominalizations*); the matrix sentence is the one into which a constituent sentence is inserted by a *generalized transformation.*" (Chomsky, 1966a:62)

MAXIMAL DOMAIN

A **maximal domain** is the phrase to which a set of phonological rules apply in order to produce a *phonological representation*.

"If a linguistic expression reaches a certain level of complexity, it will be divided into successive parts that we will call 'phonological phrases,' each of which is a **maximal domain** for phonological processes." (Chomsky and Halle, 1968:9)

"The *cyclical* application of phonological rules is repeated until the maximal domain of phonological processes is reached. The maximal domain is the 'phonological phrase,' which we assume to be marked in the *surface structure.*" (Chomsky and Halle, 1968:60)

(See example in "Cycle.")

MEANING-PRESERVING HYPOTHESIS

The **meaning-preserving hypothesis** was introduced by Katz and Postal in 1964 (*An Integrated Theory of Linguistic Description*). It states that *singulary* (obligatory) *transformations* do not change the meaning contained in the *deep structure*. "It is universally agreed that such transformations (singulary transformations) have no semantic effects, and it is clear why this must be so. The output of sentences which result from such rules is fully determined by the input P-markers." (Katz and Postal, 1964:31)

This principle is based on another principle, namely, the semantic content of a sentence is determined only by its deep structure.

MORPHEME

After discarding the term **morpheme** in favour of *formative* (in *Aspects*), Chomsky uses it again in his later work. A morpheme is essentially part of the *phrase structure* and as such, it is syntactically significant. (Chomsky, 1974)

Morphological properties refer to declensional classes, strong or weak verbs, nominalizable adjectives, etc . . . Many of these properties can be specified directly in the *lexicon* and thus "mark" a *formative* morphologically. (Chomsky, 1965:86-87)

MORPHOPHONEMICS

The **morphophonemic rules** are one of the two sets of rules composing the *phonological component* (the other set is the phonetic rules). The morphophonemic rules spell out the phonetic constitution of morphophonemes or *formatives* with respect to their specified contexts. Such rules are found in *taxonomic grammars* or *phrase-structure grammars*.

Example: take+past→/tuk/. (Chomsky, 1964b:53)

MOVEMENT

Most *transformations* have the property of changing one or several elements of a sentence from one position to another. These changes are called **movements.** An *NP* in object position can be moved to subject position, or an NP subject in an *embedded* sentence can be moved to subject position in the main clause. (See "Raising" in Appendix.) The passive transformation also involves movement.

Chomsky asserts that such rules "are permitted to move elements only to positions that precede in the hierarchy . . . The permissible rules are rules of 'upgrading' which move a noun phrase closer to the 'root of the sentence', that is, to a less embedded position." (Chomsky, 1975c:106-107)

Finally Chomsky predicts that one may reach the point when "rules can only be given in the form 'move NP,' with other conditions on their application expressed as general conditions on rules, or as properties of *initial phrase markers,* or as properties of *surface structures.*" (Chomsky, 1975c:112)

N

NESTING (See "Embedding.")

NODE

A **node** is the intersection of two branches of a *tree*. Each node corresponds to a phrase and is labelled with the name of a *category*. Each phrase or substring of S "is traceable back to a single node."

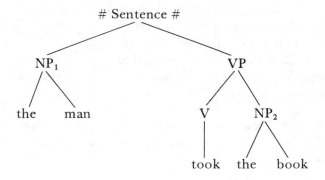

In this tree the nodes are: S, NP$_1$, VP, V, NP$_2$.

(Chomsky, 1956:113)

NOM

According to the *Standard Theory, Nom* is a nominalizing morpheme introduced by an obligatory rule which converts a declarative sentence into a noun:

$$NP - Aux - Verb - (NP) \Rightarrow NP + Possessive - nom + Verb - (of+NP)$$

Chomsky indicates that this rule "assigns to the nominalizing morpheme *nom* introduced in (the rule) the shape /ing/

when it is affixed to 'drink,' 'drive,' etc., just as it assigns to
nom the shape /æl/ when it affixed to 'refuse' and the shape
/yɨn/ when it is affixed to 'reject'." (Chomsky 1964b:76)

In "Remarks on Nominalizations", Chomsky rejects the
former theory, simplifies the content of the *transformational
component*, and suggests: "If the *lexicalist hypothesis* is correct, we should expect that derived nominals will correspond to
base structures rather than *transforms*." He then proposes the $\overline{X}$
Analysis to explain derived nominals. (Chomsky, 1970a:26)

NOUN-PHRASE (NP)

A **noun-phrase** is one of the major *constituents* of a sentence. It
can consist of a noun NP→N (Bill) or of an article and a noun
NP→T+N, or of a noun and a sentence NP→NP+S (Bill saw—the
boy who had a dog). (Chomsky, 1962a:214)

Under the *lexicalist hypothesis*, phrase *categories* are re-
analyzed as *features*; N will then be represented as $\left[\begin{smallmatrix} +N \\ -V \end{smallmatrix}\right]$.
(Chomsky, 1970a:48-52)

(See "$\overline{X}$.")

In the latest version of the *Extended Standard Theory*, NP
movement rules (preposing, and postposing) have become key.

P

PAROLE (See "Langue.")

PERFORMANCE

"The **performance** of the speaker or hearer is a complex matter
that involves many factors. One fundamental factor involved in
the speaker-hearer's performance is his knowledge of the

grammar that determines an intrinsic connection of sound and meaning for each sentence. We refer to this knowledge—for the most part, obviously, unconscious knowledge—as the speaker-hearer's *competence*. Competence, in this sense, is not to be confused with performance. Performance, that is, what the speaker-hearer actually does, is based not only on his knowledge of the language, but on many other factors as well—factors such as memory restrictions, inattention, distraction, nonlinguistic knowledge and beliefs, and so on." (Chomsky and Halle, 1968:3)

It is important to stress that performance is a direct reflection of competence only under idealized conditions, i.e., an ideal speaker-hearer in a completely homogeneous speech-community. "In actual fact it (performance) obviously could not directly reflect competence." (Chomsky, 1965:3-4)

A *performance model* is a hypothesis to produce a model of speech incorporating a grammar. Chomsky mentions the term when he refers to a discussion of Katz and Postal. (Chomsky, 1970b:70-71)

PHONES
Phones are *prime* phonetic segments. (Chomsky, 1974)

PHONETIC REPRESENTATION
"A **phonetic representation** has the form of a two-dimensional *matrix* in which the rows stand for particular *phonetic features* (such as anterior, coronal, high, low, back, etc.); the columns stand for the consecutive *segments* of the utterance generated; and the entries in the matrix determine the status of each segment with respect to the features . . . The phonetic representation of an utterance in a given language is a matrix with rows labeled by features of universal phonetics." (Chomsky and Halle, 1968:5)

The phonetic representation is the result of the application of the *phonological rules* to the *phonological representation*. Example: [sæng] and [mendid] are the phonetic representations of the past forms of "sing" and "mend." (Chomsky and Halle, 1968:11)

> **Phonetic matrix** of "inn" (Chomsky and Halle, 1968:165):

	i	n
consonantal	−	+
vocalic	+	−
nasal	2	+
tense	−	−
stress	1	−
voice	+	+
continuant	+	−

The specifications of features in phonetic representations are not necessarily binary. (See "Features.")

PHONOLOGICAL COMPONENT

The **phonological component** is the part of the *grammar* containing the rules of the sound system of a language.

"The major function of the phonological component is to derive the phonetic representation of an utterance from the surface structure assigned to it by the *syntactic component*, that is, from its representation in terms of classificatory features of the lexical items it contains, its other nonlexical *formatives*, and its analysis in term of *immediate constituents*, all of this material having been modified in an appropriate way by *readjustment rules*." (Chomsky and Halle, 1968:65)

PHONOLOGICAL MATRIX

"The entries in the phonological matrices simply indicate membership in a *category* or in its complement." (Chomsky and Halle, 1968:169)

Phonological matrix of "inn":

	i	n
consonantal	−	+
vocalic	O	O
nasal	O	+
tense	−	O
stress	O	O
voice	O	O
continuant	O	O

Phonological matrices are usually not fully specified and redundant information is not provided. (Chomsky and Halle, 1968:166)

Chomsky and Halle propose a theory of *markedness* which modifies *phonological representation*: lexical entries should not be specified + or −, but marked or unmarked. This new convention minimizes the complexity of the matrices. (Chomsky and Halle, 1968: 402-415)

PHONOLOGICAL REPRESENTATION

The representation given by the application of all readjustment rules to surface structure is referred to as the **phonological representation**. Example: [$_V$ s*ng]$_V$ and [$_V$ [$_V$ mend]$_V$ d]$_V$ are the phonological representations of the past forms of *sing* and *mend*, indicating which conversions are necessary in order to establish the proper form. (Chomsky and Halle, 1968:11)

The phonological representation is also called **phonological surface structure.** "The phonological surface structure enters the *phonological component* of the grammar and is converted by the *phonological rules* into a *phonetic representation*." (*Ibid.*:13)

PHONOLOGICAL RULES

Phonological rules convert the *phonological surface structures* into *phonetic representations*. Certain of the phonological rules will apply only to *words*; others will apply freely to *strings of* *formatives* which may be words or subpart of words, or phrases that include words. (Chomsky and Halle, 1968:12-13)

In *The Sound Pattern of English*, the authors develop a *cyclical* theory of phonological rules. (See "Cycle.")

PHRASE-MARKER

A **base phrase-marker** is the elementary unit of which a *deep structure* is constituted. It is the *structural description* of a *basic string* represented in the shape of a tree or in a bracket notation. It is generated by the base of the *syntactic component*. (Chomsky, 1965:17)

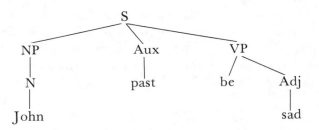

Each time a transformation applies to the base phrase-marker, there is a new phrase-marker which is called a **derived phrase-marker.**

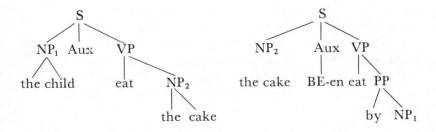

"A **generalized phrase-marker** contains all of the base phrase-markers that constitute the basis of a sentence, but it contains more information than a basis in the old sense since it also indicates explicitly how these base phrase-markers are *embedded* in one another." (Chomsky, 1965:134)

PHRASE-STRUCTURE GRAMMAR or
CONSTITUENT STRUCTURE GRAMMAR

A **phrase-structure grammar** is a *taxonomic grammar*, that is to say, it segments and classifies elements and sequences of elements. It provides an unordered set of *rewriting rules*. It remains on the level of *descriptive adequacy*.

The unordered set of rewriting rules or **phrase structure rules** which generate the syntactic structure of the *base component* are a phrase-structure grammar. (See "Base.")

> S→NP VP (read: rewrite S as NP VP)
> VP→V (NP) (read: rewrite VP as V and optional NP)
> NP→(Det)(Adj)N (read: rewrite NP as optional Det, optional Adj, and N)
> etc.

PORT-ROYAL GRAMMAR

The **Port-Royal Grammar**, written by Lancelot and Arnauld at Port-Royal in the XVIIth century, was the first philosophical grammar. Chomsky considers that it opened up the way for modern linguistics. In *Cartesian Linguistics*, he analyzes the contribution of that grammar on his theory: creative aspect of language use, notion of *deep* and *surface structure, universal principles of grammar*, study of human language linked to speculations on the human mind.

"Thus a fully adequate psychology requires the postulation of a 'creative principle' alongside of the 'mechanical principle' that suffices to account for all other aspects of the inanimate and animate world and for a significant range of human actions and 'passions' as well." (Chomsky, 1966b:6)

". . . We can formulate a second fundamental conclusion of Cartesian linguistics, namely, that deep and surface structures need not be identical. The underlying organization of a sentence relevant to semantic interpretation is not necessarily revealed by the actual arrangement and phrasing of its given components." (*Ibid.*:33)

"The central doctrine of Cartesian linguistics is that the general features of grammatical structure are common to all languages and reflect certain fundamental properties of the mind. It is this assumption which led the philosophical grammarians to concentrate on *grammaire générale* rather than *grammaire particulière*." (*Ibid.*:59)

POST-LEXICAL STRUCTURE

"Post-lexical structures are *mapped* into *semantic representations* by the *semantic rules*. In this formulation, the post-lexical structures are called *Deep Structures*." (Chomsky, 1970a:65) In other words, they are structures to which the lexical insertion rules have applied.

PRESUPPOSITION (See "Focus.")

PRIMES

Primes are primitive symbols which appear in a representation. They are indivisible elements. For instance, at the level of word representation, *the, man* are primes; at the level of *phonetic representation, phones* are prime phonetic *segments*. (Chomsky, 1974)

PROPER ANALYSIS (See "Analyzability.")

The subdivision of the *phrase-marker* P, of a *terminal string* S, into successive elements $s_1, \ldots s_n$ each s_i traceable to a *node* in P, is called the **proper analysis** of the terminal string S with respect to P. (Chomsky, 1961a:131)

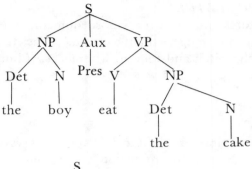

```
S
NP Aux VP
Det N Aux V NP
etc.
```

PROPER INCLUSION

In mathematics, in the set theory, one says that a set A is **properly contained** in a set B if all the elements of A are in B, but A and B are not identical. According to Chomsky, a phrase is properly contained in a *noun-phrase* if it is one of the elements of that noun-phrase.

> Example: Comp [NP [S COMP John saw what]] surprised Mary

The internal *COMP* is properly contained in the bracketed *NP* which is a subject phrase. (Chomsky, 1973:249)

The notion of proper inclusion is not restricted to NPs.

```
                    Det
        ┌────────────┼────────────┐
     Preart          of          Poss
        │                  ┌───────┴───────┐
     several              NP               S
                           │
                         John
```
(Chomsky, 1970a:36-37)

(In this case, NP is properly contained in Det.)

PROSODIC FEATURE

"Prosodic features are features whose domain extends over sequences that are longer than a word." The term refers essentially to the pitch and tone of utterances. (Chomsky and Halle, 1968:68)

PRUNING

Pruning is a principle enunciated by Ross. It says that if an *embedded node* S does not immediately *dominate* at least two nodes it can be *deleted* or pruned. (Ross, 1967:26) For instance, the following structure:

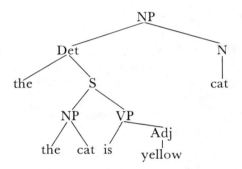

can be transformed, by Relative Clause Reduction, and give the derived phrase marker:

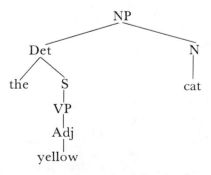

According to the pruning principle the S node must be deleted.

Q

QUANTIFIER

In mathematics and in logic, a **quantifier** is a term that indicates a quantity in a precise statement: *some, all, every*. The quantifiers are either universal quantifiers: "for all x ... " or existential quantifiers: "there is an x such that . . . . " By extension a quantifier is considered, by the linguists, as a determiner which expresses any type of quantity: *the, many, much, several, few*, as well as numeral expressions. Chomsky even includes *wh-* "as a kind of quantifier". (Chomsky, 1975c:93)

A *NP* is said to be quantified when it is accompanied by a quantifier.

Quantification is the operation by which a NP is quantified.

Chomsky agrees with Jackendoff who claims that quantifiers (like *negation*) belong to the semantic structure and as such are determined by *surface structure*. (Jackendoff, 1972:16)

R

RECOVERABILITY OF DELETION

The **recoverability condition on deletion** indicates that "a deletion operation can eliminate only a *dummy element*, or a formative explicitly mentioned in the *structure index* (for example, *you* in imperatives), or the designated representative of a category ... or an element that is otherwise represented in the sentence in a fixed position." (Chomsky, 1965: 144-145)

"We have mentioned in several places (Chapter 3, notes 1 and 13, and pp. 144f.) that deletions must be recoverable, and have suggested that this condition can be formalized by the following convention relating to what we called '*erasure transformations*': an erasure transformation can use a term X of its *proper analysis* to erase a term Y of the proper analysis only if X and Y are identical." (Chomsky, 1965:177)

For example, the rule of *agent deletion* states that, in a passive sentence the agent can be deleted only if it is the indefinite pronoun, *someone* or *something*. In the sentence:

The case will be examined

the deleted agent (if there is no context) can be understood only as: by someone.

ROOT

The **root** node of a sentence is the highest *node* in a phrase-marker; it is the S node.

A **root sentence** is the matrix sentence, that is to say, the structures immediately dominated by the highest S.

Root transformations are transformations which apply at the level of the matrix sentence. Question and Imperative transformations are, in English, root transformations. Such rules "do not apply to *embedded sentences*, but only to the full sentence structure." (Chomsky, 1975c:84)

"A root transformation (RT) is one in which any constituents moved, inserted or copied are immediately dominated by a root (node) in the derived structure." (Edmonds, 69:7)

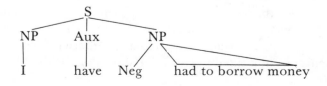

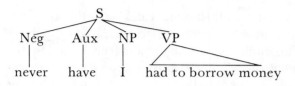

RULES, READJUSTMENT

"The **readjustment rules** provide a link between the syntactic and the *phonological components* of the grammar." (Chomsky and Halle, 1968:61)

"It seems that in general these modifications involve elimination of structure, that is, deletion of *nodes* or of *paired brackets.*" (Chomsky and Halle, 1968:10)

"The readjustment rules will modify the *surface structure* in various ad hoc ways, demarcating it into phonological phrases, eliminating some structure, and replacing some occurences of # by +." (*Ibid.*:13)

$$\text{Example: } t \longrightarrow [\text{+voice}] \; / = \begin{Bmatrix} \text{mi} \underline{\quad} + \text{ive} \\ \text{ver} \underline{\quad} + \text{ion} \end{Bmatrix}$$

(Read: t becomes a voiced consonant (+voice) in the context (/—) submit+ive or in the context subvert+ion)

"This will account for the spirantization of /t/ in *sub-missive* .... and the voicing of /t/ in *subversion* with subsequent devoicing." (See discussion in Chomsky and Halle, 1968:223f.)

RULES, REDUNDANCY

"The **redundancy rules** both phonological and syntactic, state general properties of all *lexical entries.*

"The real function of the *phonological redundancy rules* is to determine the class of phonologically admissible (though perhaps not occurring) sequences in a principled way." (Chomsky, 1965:168-169)

"Those readjustment rules which have the effect of restricting the class of possible lexical entries by eliminating certain possibilities we shall sometimes designate as **lexical redundancy rules.**" They apply within a single lexical entry and simply fill in unspecified squares of *phonological matrices*, without violating *invariance*. These rules express regularities of lexical classification. (Chomsky and Halle, 1968: 163/171)
(See discussion *Ibid.* :380-389)

RULES, REWRITING

Rewriting rules or *phrase-structure rules* are instructions contained in the *base* of the *grammar*:

> S→NP VP
> VP→V (NP)
> NP→ (Det)(Adj) N
> etc.

(Read the symbol → as: is to be rewritten as . . .)
Rewriting rules are either *context-free* as they are found in the *base*, or *context-sensitive* like: "A→Z/X—Y, where X and Y are (possibly null) *strings of symbols*, A is a single category symbol, and Z is a nonnull string of symbols. This rule is interpreted as asserting that the category A is realized as the string Z when it is in the environment consisting of X to the left and Y to the right. Application of the rewriting rule to a string . . . XAY . . . converts this to the string . . . XZY . . . " (Chomsky, 1965:66)

RULE OF GRAMMAR

"By a *grammar* of the language L I will mean a device of some sort (that is, a set of **rules**) that provides, at least, a complete specification of an infinite set of grammatical sentences of L and their *structural descriptions* . . . Among the rules of a grammar there are some that play a part in the generation of an infinite set of *strings*, each of which is an essentially ortho-graphic representation of some grammatical sentence. These are called *syntactic rules* . . . Other rules, called *morphophonemic*, convert a *terminal string* into the phonetic description of an utterance . . . " (Chomsky, 1961a:119-121)

RULE ORDERING

The ordering of rules is of crucial importance and *generative grammars* require **extrinsic order** as well as **intrinsic order**.

"If a certain *transformation* T_1 applies to a certain structure that is formed only by application of T_2, there is an intrinsic order T_1, T_2." (Chomsky 1965:223) In other words, given two rules, they are intrinsically ordered if one can apply only after the other has applied. This is the case for example, in English, of *passive* and *affix hopping,* or negation and *contraction.*

On the other hand, if two rules are ordered, but not intrinsically, they are said to be extrinsically ordered. This is the case of *negation* and *question,* for instance. [Extrinsic order has been a much debated issue; see Koutsoudas (1972 and 1973), Lehman (1972), Ringen (1972) and others.]

Rules are said to be in a **linear order** when they apply in sequence and in a fixed order. (Chomsky and Halle, 1968:18-21)

"Two rules are **disjunctively ordered** in the sense that if one applies the other is not permitted to apply. Thus a sequence of rules abbreviated in terms of the parenthesis notation con-stitutes a disjunctively ordered block; as soon as one of these rules is applied the remaining rules are skipped within any one *cycle* of a derivation." (Chomsky and Halle, 1968:30)

Obviously, **conjunctive ordering** refers to cases where all rules can apply one after the other. (*Ibid.*:77)

S

SCHEMA

A **schema** is a certain kind of expression "constructed from the symbols that appear in *rules* and certain auxiliary expressions." (Chomsky and Halle, 1968:393)

The precise definition is rather complicated (see *Ibid.*: 392-393), but it involves the "collapsing" of a sequence of rules into a "schema" and the "expanding" of a schema into a collection of rules. These collapsing and expanding are axiomatically defined (p.394). "For each sequence of rules there will be some schema that expands into this sequence and that is optimal in the sense that it contains a minimal number of *feature* occurrences. The number of feature occurrences in the optimal schema will be the value of the original sequence of rules. In this way, each sequence of rules is assigned an integral value, and grammars can be compared with respect to the degree to which they achieve linguistically significant *generalization.*" (*Ibid.*:393)

"In informal discussion, when no confusion can arise, (Chomsky and Halle do not) maintain the distinction between the term 'rule' and 'schema' extending 'rule' to schemata as well." (*Ibid.*: 333)

Example: "V → [1 stress] / X —C_0 (W) / — (+affix)]"

where W is a weak cluster, C_0 is a string of zero or more consonants, and X does not contain an internal # boundary."

This schema is a "collapsing" of the following sequence of rules:

(a)   V → 1[stress] / X ___C_0 W+affix]
(b)   V → 1[stress] / X ___C_0 +affix]
(c)   V → 1[stress] / X ___C_0 W]
(d)   V → 1[stress] / X ___C_0]

(*Ibid.*:32-33)

SCOPE

Scope belongs to the domain of *semantic interpretation* and Chomsky uses the term with the meaning given by Jackendoff. Some verbs induce a certain ambiguity about their referents; the area of ambiguity is called the scope. The example given is: "John wants to catch a fish." *A fish* may be semantically ambiguous because it does not refer to a specific fish as long as John has not caught one.

Chomsky and Jackendoff agree that scope is not only determined by a class of verbs but also by some modal operators, *quantifiers*, or logical particles. (Jackendoff, 1972:280-281) (Chomsky, 1975c:104-105)

SEGMENTS

In phonology, the consonants and vowels that constitute a *formative* are called **segments**. ". . . They are formally treated as complexes of *features* rather than as further unanalyzable entities." (Chomsky and Halle, 1968:335)

"The segmental features are given in the universal theory of language and have universal phonetic correlates." (Chomsky and Halle: 364)

SEMANTIC COMPONENT

"The **semantic component** of the grammar is a system of rules that assigns a *semantic interpretation* to each syntactic description, making essential reference to the *deep structure* and possibly taking into account certain aspects of *surface structure* as well." (Chomsky and Halle, 1968:6-7)

SEMANTIC FEATURES

"**Semantic features** constitute a well-defined set in a given grammar. A feature belongs to this set just in case it is not referred to by any rule of the *phonological* or *syntactic component*." (Chomsky, 1965:88)

Example: "It was an intriguing plan." The *structural description* of this sentence contains the *terminal string* under-

lying "the plan intrigued one (i.e., unspecified) human" . . .
This fact might be suggested as the explanation for the cited
semantic feature.

In general, as syntactic description becomes deeper, what
appear to be semantic questions fall increasingly within its
scope; . . . it seems clear that *explanatory adequacy* for
descriptive semantics requires, beyond this, the development of
an independent semantic theory . . ." (Chomsky, 1964b:77)

SEMANTIC INTERPRETATION

Semantic interpretation is determined by: the meaning of
the *formatives,* the analysis of their combinations in the *surface
structure* and of the *syntactic component* of the *deep structure.*
"The meaning of a sentence is based on the meaning of its
elementary parts and the manner of their combination. It is
clear that the manner of combination provided by the *surface
structure* is in general almost totally irrelevant to semantic
interpretation, whereas the grammatical relations expressed in
the abstract *deep structure* are, in many cases, just those that
determine the meaning of the sentence." (Chomsky, 1965:162)

According to what Chomsky calls the *Standard Theory,*
a system of rules of semantic interpretation applies to the *base*
of the grammar. "Deep structures determine *semantic representation* under the rules of semantic interpretation."
(Chomsky, 1972b:65-66)

In the *Extended Standard Theory,* "semantic interpretation is held to be determined by the pair (deep structure,
surface structure) of Σ, rather than by the deep structure
alone." (Chomsky, 1972b:134)

SEMANTIC PRIMITIVE

In a general sense a primitive is a figure or a form from which
another is derived. A **semantic primitive** is the basic notion
underlying a lexical item. For instance, "brother of (father-
or-mother)" is the semantic primitive of *uncle.* (Chomsky,
1972b:73)

SEMANTIC UNIT

A **semantic unit** is an expression like "take advantage," which, in a *structural index* is placed under a single *node*, or single *nonterminal*, which cannot be subdivided into other *categories*. (Chomsky, 1973:236)

SEMIOTICS

Chomsky uses the word **semiotics** as the vaguest possible term to refer to some general theory of language use. (Chomsky, 1974)

S or Σ

S is the label of a sentence.

In earlier work, Chomsky refers to a sentence within *boundary* signs: #Sentence# as **Σ**.

SORTAL PREDICATE

Chomsky suggests the classification of namable things according to their "internal structure, constitution, origin, function (for artifacts), and other properties. This is not to say that we necessarily know the defining structure, and so on, but that we assume that it exists and that new entities are assigned correctly to the 'sort' and designated by the *sortal predicate* just in case they share the 'essential properties,' whatever they are." (Chomsky, 1975c:44-45)

SPECIFIED SUBJECT

A **subject** is said to be **specified** or lexically specified if it is represented by a lexical item such as, *Bill, the man* or by a referring pronoun, *he, they*. Example: I wondered if Bill would come, or, I wondered if he would come. (Chomsky, 1973:255)

A *trace* can also be a specified subject. (See "Trace.")

The **specified subject condition** (SSC) is a constraint of considerable importance which has been explicated in Chomsky

(1973a:250ff) and which is formulated as follows: "In a structure of the form [... X ... [Z—WYV] ...], no rule can relate X and Y if Z is the subject of WYV and is not controlled by X." (Chomsky, 1975c:150)

STANDARD THEORY

The **standard theory** is outlined in Chomsky (1965). "It assumes that in addition to a *lexicon,* a system of *grammatical trans-formations,* and a system of phonological rules, the *grammar* contains a system of rules of *semantic interpretation* and a context-free *categorial component* with a designated terminal element Δ. The categorial component and the lexicon are referred to as *The Base* of the grammar." It also states that "*surface structures* are mapped into *phonetic repre-sentations* by the phonological rules. *Post-lexical structures* are *mapped* into *semantic representation* by the semantic rules. In this formulation, the post-lexical structures are called *deep-structures.*" (Chomsky, 1972:65)

(See "Extended Standard Theory.")

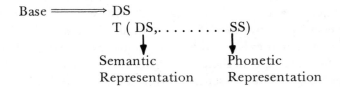

$$\text{Base} \Longrightarrow \text{DS}$$
$$\text{T (DS,} \ldots \ldots \ldots \text{SS)}$$

| Semantic | Phonetic |
| Representation | Representation |

STRESS

For discussion of the various rules,
    alternating stress rule
    contrastive stress
    main stress rule
    nuclear stress rule
    primary stress rule
    stress adjustment rule
    stress contour

stress placement rule
stressed syllable rule

see *The Sound Pattern of English.*

STRING

A **string** is formed by a linear sequence of symbols linked together by an operation called *concatenation* and symbolized by +. (Chomsky, 1957:109)

(a)   *tele+graph* is a *formative string*

(b)   *we+establish+past+tele+graph+ic+communicate+ion*   is a string of formatives or a **full string.** (Chomsky and Halle, 1968:9)

(c)   A **basic string** is the string generated by the *base* of the *syntactic component*; "it is associated with a *structural description* called a *base phrase-marker.*" (Chomsky, 1965: 17)

(d)   A **pre-terminal string** is a string that consists of *grammatical formatives* and *complex symbols;* "it is generated by the *branching rules* of the *categorial component.*" (Chomsky, 1965:122)

Example:
[+N, −Count, +Abstract] M̂ Q̂ the
      [+N, +Count, +Animate, +Human]

(e)   A **terminal string** is the last line of a *derivation*, when all the *rewriting rules* have successively applied. "The final string or terminal string consists only of *formatives* and therefore no further rewriting is possible." (Chomsky, 1965:66)

(f)   A **maximal string** contains no inner brackets. Example: *board eraser* is a maximal string after certain rules have been applied. (Chomsky and Halle, 1968:15)

A **derivable language** is a set of *strings* that can be derived from some grammar $[\Sigma, F]$. Σ = sentence, F= set of instruction formulas.

A **terminal language** is the set of *terminal strings* from some system $[\Sigma, F]$. (Chomsky, 1956:112)

STRUCTURAL CHANGE

A **structural change** is produced by a *transformation*. The elements of a *string*, labelled and segmented by a *structural analysis* (or structural description), are re-arranged according to the rule applied. The structural change produced by the passive *transformation* coincides with the following formula:

Structural analysis: $\quad$ NP $\quad$ Aux $\quad$ V $\quad$ NP

$\qquad\qquad\qquad\quad X_1 \qquad X_2 \qquad X_3 \qquad X_4 \Rightarrow$

Structural change: $\quad X_4 \qquad X_2$ +be+en X_3 by+X_1

(See "Transformation.") $\qquad$ (Chomsky, 1957:112)

STRUCTURAL CONDITION

The **structural condition** of a *transformation* specifies the nature of the syntactic environment in which a transformation can apply. For instance, the reflexive transformation applies only if the two *NPs* are identical:

NP–VP–NP

1 $\quad$ 2 $\quad$ 3 $\rightarrow$ 1 $\quad$ 2 $\quad$ Refl. condition:1=3

STRUCTURAL DESCRIPTION or
STRUCTURAL ANALYSIS

A *tree* represents the **structural description** of a sentence into *immediate constituents*. Such a representation of a sentence is called a *phrase-marker*. Each *node* of the *tree* represents a constituent. The top of the tree represents the highest constituent (the sentence S). The terminal nodes are the smallest syntactic units (the *morphemes*).

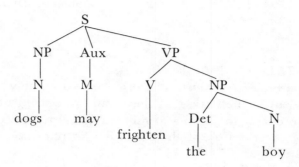

The structural description of a sentence analyzes the sentence in terms of its *syntactic structure*. It is the basic step which defines which *transformations* can apply in order to obtain a *structural change*. The optional passive transformation can apply, in the following example, given the **structural analysis**.

$$\text{Structural analysis:} \quad NP - \quad Aux - V - NP$$
$$X_1 - \quad X_2 - X_3 - X_4 - \implies$$
$$\text{Structural change:} \quad X_4 - X_2 + be + en - X_3 - by + X_1$$

STRUCTURAL FEATURE
The **structural features** of a *string* are specified in the *syntactic component* of a *generative grammar*. They are the set of information concerning a particular string: "... how it is subdivided into *constituents* and what are the *categories* to which these substrings belong." (Chomsky, 1964b:83)

STRUCTURAL INDEX
Structural index is another term for *structural analysis* or *structural description*. (Chomsky, 1965:122)

STRUCTURAL LINGUISTICS
Structural linguistics (*taxonomic* or *phrase structure* linguistics) describes utterances contained in a corpus, by a method of classification and segmentation. The rules it formulates remain on the level of the *surface structure*. (Chomsky, 1965:5)

STRUCTURE-DEPENDENT
"*Grammatical transformations* are invariably **structure-dependent** in the sense that they apply to a *string* of *words* (or more properly to a string of minimal linguistic units) by virtue of the organization of these words into phrases." (Chomsky, 1972a:61)

STRUCTURE-PRESERVING HYPOTHESIS
This theory is due to Emonds (1970) and predicts that: "All movement rules among the *cyclic transformations* are '**structure-preserving**,' in that items of *category* X can only be moved to a position *dominated* by the category X. Thus *Noun-Phrases* can be moved to a Noun-Phrase position, etc." (Chomsky, 1975d:23)

Accordingly, the result of a transformation is a type of structure very similar to the structure *generated* by the base rules.

SUBCATEGORIZATION RULE
"A **subcategorization rule** introduces *syntactic features* and thus forms or extends a *complex symbol* . . . Subcategorization rules may be *context-free* or *context-sensitive* . . . The subcategorization rules that are context-free are, in effect, strictly local *transformational rules*."

The subcategorization rules can be divided into two types, namely: (1) the **strict subcategorization rules** which specify the possible *categories* of the context in which a symbol may appear.

Example:

$$V \rightarrow CS/\text{---} \left\{ \begin{array}{l} NP \\ \# \\ Adj. \\ \cdot \\ \cdot \\ \cdot \end{array} \right.$$

(2) the **selectional rules** which specify the *syntactic features* of the frames in which a symbol, verb or adjective, may appear.

Example:

$$[+V] \rightarrow CS/ \left\{ \begin{array}{l} [\pm Abstract] \quad Aux \text{---} \\ \text{---} Det \, [\pm Animate] \end{array} \right.$$

(Chomsky, 1965:112-113)

SUBJACENCY

"If X is superior to Y in a phrase-marker P, then Y is **'subjacent'** to X if there is at most one *cyclic* category $C \neq Y$ such that C contains Y and C does not contain X . . . in the sentence:

COMP he believes [$_S$ COMP John saw who]

who is subjacent to both *nodes COMP.*" (See discussion, Chomsky, 1973:247.)

The principle of subjacency states that transformations must apply to positions at the same level of the cycle or in adjacent levels. "A transformation may not move an item within the cyclic category A to a position within the cyclic category C that includes category B including A and included in C." (Chomsky, 1975c:85)

Example: the underlying structure (1) cannot give sentence (2)

1) [$_{NP}$ the only one that I like of Tolstoy's novels] is out of print

2) [NP[NP the only one] of Tolstoy's novels] is out of print
that I like

SUBJECT/GRAMMATICAL SUBJECT/ LOGICAL SUBJECT

In the sentence "I persuaded John to be examined by a specialist," "John" is the direct object of the VP as well as the **grammatical subject** of the *embedded* sentence. The underlying *deep-structure* is: I—persuaded—John—a specialist will examine John—

In the sentence "I persuaded a specialist to examine John," "a specialist" is the direct object of the VP and the **logical subject** of the embedded sentence. The underlying deep-structure is: I—persuaded—a specialist—a specialist will examine John. (Chomsky, 1965:23)

The grammatical subject is the subject of a clause in the *surface structure*. The logical subject is the subject of a clause in the deep structure.

The **formal subject** of a sentence is the NP directly *dominated* by S.

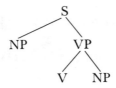

SUPERIORITY

"The *category* A is **superior** to the category B, in a *phrase-marker*, if every *major category dominating* A dominates B as well but not conversely." (Chomsky, 1973:246 and note 27)

SURFACE STRUCTURE

The **surface structure** is composed of the actual sentences of the language, the sentences speakers actually produce.

"The surface structure refers to a representation of the phrases that constitute a linguistic expression and the *categories* to which these phrases belong. 'John is certain to leave'. The surface structure includes the verb phrases 'to leave' and 'is certain to leave'; but the surface structure includes no proposition of the form 'John will leave' even though this proposition expresses part of the meaning of 'John is certain to leave'." (Chomsky, 1972a:105)

"The *rules* of syntax *generate* surface structures and a universal principle of interpretation assigns the *boundary symbol* # in certain places. The *readjustment rules* modify the surface structure in various ad hoc ways. The abstract object thus constructed (*phonological surface structure*) enters the *phonological component* of the grammar and is converted by the *phonological rules* into a *phonetic representation.*"(Chomsky and Halle, 1968:13)

SYNTACTIC COMPONENT

"The **syntactic component** consists of rules that *generate deep structures* combined with rules mapping these into associated *surface structures* . . . These two systems of rules are the *base* and the *transformational components* of the syntax respectively." (Chomsky, 1972a:140)

SYNTACTIC FEATURES

Syntactic features form a large class. They can be classified according to the information they give about a lexical item.

(a) **Category features** indicate which grammatical category a *formative* belongs to: [± Noun], [± Adjective], [± Verb].

(b) **Contextual features** indicate the position of the *formative* within the syntagmatic structure. A transitive verb will have the contextual feature [− NP], a verb like *feel* will be specified [− Adj].

(c) **Inherent features** indicate [± Animate] for instance.

(d) **Selectional features** refer to the specific features assigned
     to the context in which a symbol may appear. They
     indicate, for instance, what kind of subject or object a
     certain verb is supposed to have. The lexical entry for
     drink will be: [+animate] — [−animate]

(e) **Strict subcategorization features** specify, in terms of
     category, the frame of *constituents* within which a
     formative can be inserted; example: eat (+−NP).

In "Remarks on Nominalization," Chomsky develops the
lexicalist theory and suggests replacing the base rules intro-
ducing N, A and V "by a schema where in place of . . . there
appears the full range of structures that serve as complements
and X can be any one of N, A or V:

$$\overline{X} \rightarrow X \ldots "$$ (Chomsky, 1970a:52)

SYNTACTIC RULES
"Among the rules of a grammar there are some that play a part
in the generation of an infinite set of *strings*, each of which is an
essentially orthographic representation of some grammatical
sentence. These we will call **syntactic rules**; the final result of
applying only these, we will call a *terminal string*." (Chomsky,
1961a:121)

SYNTACTIC STRUCTURE
The **syntactic structure** refers to the internal organization
of a *string*. It is the description of its grammatical construction.
   A **syntactic description** indicates the *grammatical relations*
and *functions* of the various elements of a sentence.

T

TAXONOMIC LINGUISTICS

"**Taxonomic linguistics** is empiricist in its assumption that general linguistic theory consists only of a body of procedures for determining the *grammar* of a language from a corpus of data."

Taxonomic linguistics holds the view "that *syntactic structure* is determined exclusively by operations of segmentations and classification." (Chomsky, 1965:52-88)

TENSED-S CONDITION

Tensed-S condition (tensed-S stands for a tensed sentence, i.e., a sentence with a verb in a particular tense, present, past or future) makes the claim that no element of the finite *embedded* sentence can be extracted from or inserted into that sentence by a *transformation*. This condition is generalized as follows:

"No rule can involve X, Y in the structure

$$\dots X \dots [_\alpha \dots Y \dots] \dots$$

where α is a tensed sentence." (Chomsky, 1973:238)

The only permissible extraction from a tensed-S is when an item in the *COMP* of a tensed-S moves into the COMP of a higher S.

TERMINAL SYMBOL

A **terminal symbol** is a *morpheme*; it is the smallest syntactic unit. It does not appear on the left-hand side of the arrow in any *base rule*. (In other words, this means that it cannot expand.) A terminal symbol is represented by Δ; "it indicates the position in which an item from the *lexicon* may appear." (Chomsky, 1972a:143)

In a *structural description*, a terminal symbol is a lexical item (*sincerity, boy*). A **nonterminal symbol** is a *category* and it labels a *node*.

The nonterminal elements may be S (sentence) or the elements "that stand for lexical categories, in particular N (for 'noun'), V (for 'verb'), Adj (for 'adjective') . . . A nonterminal symbol or a *lexical category* A can appear on the left-hand side of a rule A → Z only if Z is Δ (that is to say a terminal symbol)." (Chomsky, 1972a:143)

THEMATIC RELATIONS

This term is due to Richard Stanley. Chomsky suggests that **thematic relations** are notions such as Agent, Goal, Instrument. "That one central element in *semantic interpretation* is determined by *deep structures* and the lexical items that appear in them." (Chomsky, 1975a:108)

In *Reflections on Language*, Chomsky modifies this position and claims that owing to the *trace theory, surface structures* can be taken "to be the sole elements that enter into semantic interpretation." He now considers thematic relations to be determined by surface structure. (Chomsky, 1975c:117)

The theory of thematic relations has been developed most explicitly in Jackendoff (1972).

THEORY OF LEARNING

In a general discussion about cognitive capacity, Chomsky gives a tentative definition of what a **learning theory** (LT) could be. "The learning theory for humans in the domain of language will be the system of principles by which humans arrive at knowledge of language, given linguistic experience, that is, given a preliminary analysis that they develop for the data of language." (Chomsky, 1975c:14)

It is obvious that *universal grammar* (UG) is "a significant component of LT(H, L)," i.e., of a human language. (*Ibid.*:29)

TRACE

When a NP moves, a **trace** (**t**) is left in the position from which it has moved. A trace is a *variable* controlled by the NP. It can be a *specified subject*. Even though it is phonologically null, a trace affects a *semantic rule* as strongly as an expressed subject.

The **trace theory** of movement rule states that "when a transformation moves a phrase P from position X to position Y it leaves in position X a trace bound by P." (Chomsky, 1975c:95)

Example: Y seems $|_s$ John to be a nice fellow]
John seems $[_s$ t to be a nice fellow]

"The position of the *bound trace* in surface structure allows us to determine the grammatical relation of 'John' as subject of the *embedded* sentence." (Chomsky, 1975c:96)

Chomsky claims that the trace theory facilitates semantic interpretation by restricting it to *surface structure*. He further suggests that the trace theory (along with the specified subject condition) may be part of *universal grammar*. (Chomsky, 1975c:97, 103)

TRANSFORM

Transform—a term used by Harris before Chomsky—is the sentence obtained after a *transformation* has applied to a *phrase-marker*, or to another sentence. (Chomsky, 1962a:229)

TRANSFORMATION

Transformations convert one *string* A to a string B by deleting, moving, adding, or substituting constituents. The initial string which is transformed may be:

(a)   a *base* structure such as:

a bird—present—sing

which. submitted to the *transformation Number-Agreement* reads:

A bird sings.

Such transformations which apply to strings that are not acceptable utterances to produce acceptable sentences, or in other words, transformations which apply to *deep structures* to give *surface structures*, are called obligatory. The result is a *kernel sentence*.

(b)   a kernel sentence such as:

Cats eat mice

can be transformed by the *Passive rule* into:

Mice are eaten by cats.

Such transformations are called optional. They produce *derived sentences*.

Transformations that operate on single phrase-markers are called **singulary transformations**. Singulary transformations operate on "constituent sentences before they are embedded, and on matrix sentences after embedding has taken place." (Chomsky, 1965:135)

(c)   pairs of strings. Such operations are called **generalized transformations**. Generalized transformations "operate on a set of *P-markers* (probably two) to produce a single new derived P-marker by embedding part or all of one in the other or by conjoining the two in some way." (Katz and Postal, 1964:12)

Example: The apple is red/ the apple is on the table

If the *Relative transformation* applies, the new sentence is:

The apple which is on the table is red.

In the *Extended Standard Theory*, the distinction between generalized and singulary transformations is no longer necessary on account of the recursion in the base.

Each transformational rule has two parts:

(a)   a *structural description* (SD) which enumerates the essential elements in the order they occur;
(b)   a *structural change* (SC) which indicates the reordering, deletion, substitution, or addition involved in the process.

Sometimes a third part is added containing a condition.

Major transformations generally involve movement and bring radical changes to a string. Relativization and passive are among the major transformations. (See "Housekeeping rules" and *Root transformations* under "Root.")

According to Chomsky's theory, a transformation, generally, is a single valued operation, that is to say, one transformation produces one result. In some cases, two transformations are very closely related in the sense that the SDs of the strings to which they apply are the same for one as for the other. This is what is called a **family of transformations.** Interrogation and negation are related in that manner.

A **transformation marker** represents the transformational structure of an utterance; in other words, it represents the transformational history by which a sentence is derived from its base. (Chomsky, 1965:131)

TRANSFORMATIONAL GENERATIVE GRAMMAR

A **transformational generative grammar** "consists of a finite sequence of context-restricted *rewriting rules* $\varphi \rightarrow \psi$ and a finite number of *transformational rules*, together with a statement of the restrictions on the order of application of these *trans-*

formations. The result of a transformation is, in general, available for further transformation, so that an indefinite number of *P-markers*, of quite varied kinds, can be generated by repeated application of transformations." (Chomsky, 1961a:136)

TRANSFORMATIONAL GRAMMAR

A **transformational grammar,** according to the pattern of Harris, is a development of *taxonomic grammar*. It shows, by means of discourse analysis, how two or more *strings* have symmetrical relations.

$$\text{The gift pleased John} - \text{John was pleased by the gift}$$
$$N_1 - V - N_2 \longleftrightarrow N_2 -be- V - by\ N_1$$

This allows the linguist to find structural regularity, but it offers no recursive procedure to produce new sentences. (Chomsky, 1974)

"The central idea of transformational grammar (as developed by Chomsky), is that *deep* and *surface structures* are, in general, distinct and that the surface structure is determined by repeated application of certain formal operations called '*grammatical transformations*' to objects of a more elementary sort." (Chomsky, 1965:16)

TRANSPARENCY

The property of **transparency** permits *noun phrases* to be extracted from a larger noun phrase in which they are contained.

Example: "John thought Bill had read the book."

The NP *the book* can be extracted from the NP *Bill had read the book* by a question formation "What book did John think Bill . . . " (Chomsky, 1972a:54f)

Chomsky used the term in *Language and Mind*, but has discarded it since.

TREE

A **tree** is one of the possible representations of a *phrase-marker*, or the *structural description* of a sentence. The root of the tree is labelled with the symbol S which stands for sentence. Each *node* is labelled with the name of a *category*: NP, VP, N, V, etc. . . The end points of the branches are labelled with the symbols of the *terminal string*. (Chomsky, 1961a:121/ 1964b:82)

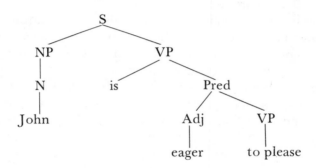

Under the current theory of *syntactic categories* developed in "Remarks on Nominalization," trees are no longer represented as NP, VP, but as N, A, V, or even $\bar{X}$.

U

UNIVERSALS

Language universals are the nonaccidental features and properties that all languages have in common.

Philosophical or **universal grammar** originates in the *Grammaire générale et raisonnée* of Port Royal. "Universal grammar constitutes an explanatory theory of a much deeper sort than particular grammar . . . The study of universal grammar, so understood, is a study of the nature of human intellectual capacities. It tries to formulate the necessary and sufficient conditions that a system must meet to qualify as a potential human language, conditions that are rooted in the human 'language capacity', and thus constitute the innate organization that determines what counts as linguistic experience and what knowledge of language arises on the basis of this experience." (Chomsky, 1972a:27)

"Let us define 'universal grammar' (UG) as the system of principles, conditions, and rules that are elements or properties of all human languages not merely by accident but by (biological) necessity." (Chomsky, 1975c:29)

"**Formal universals** involve the character of the rules that appear in grammars and the ways in which they can be interconnected." (Chomsky, 1965:29)

"A theory of **substantive universals** claims that items of a particular kind in any language must be drawn from a fixed class of items . . . Substantive universals concern the vocabulary for the description of language." (Chomsky, 1965:28-29)

UNIVERSAL PHONETIC ALPHABET

"The **universal phonetic alphabet** is part of a universal phonetic theory. The symbols of this alphabet are specified in terms of a set of *phonetic features* . . . The symbols of the universal phonetic are mere conventional abbreviations for sets of feature specifications." (Chomsky, 1964b:86)

UNLIKE-SUBJECT CONSTRAINT

In some complement constructions, "the subject of the *embedded* sentence must not be identical to the subject of the *matrix sentence*." This principle, demonstrated by Rosenbaum (1967), has been illustrated by Perlmutter (1971:4-9) who calls it the **unlike-subject constraint**. Example:

> I screamed for Clyde to commit himself.
> *I screamed for me to commit myself.
> *I screamed to commit myself.

UNSPECIFIED SUBJECT

In a *deep structure*, an **unspecified subject** is a *dummy element* which stands as the subject of an *embedded* sentence, and is referred to as PRO.

> Example: We heard about plans [PRO to kill Bill]

> (Chomsky, 1973:255)

UTTERANCE

Chomsky uses the word **utterance** in the usual sense; it is any type of spoken expression. "The term utterance belongs naturally to the theory of *performance*. Utterances are the items that constitute the linguist's corpus, the 'primary linguistic data' for the language-learner." (Chomsky, 1974b:39)

V

VARIABLE

The letters of the Greek alphabet (α,β, etc.) are used as values of *features*. For example, [α person] means first, second or third person, according as α takes the value first, second or third. And [β plural] means singular in case β is $-$, and means plural if β is $+$. As an example, the rule of number agreement

$$\begin{matrix} \text{NP} & - & \text{tense} \\ \begin{bmatrix} \alpha & \text{person} \\ \beta & \text{plural} \end{bmatrix} \end{matrix} \implies \begin{matrix} \text{NP} & - & \text{tense} \\ \begin{bmatrix} \alpha & \text{person} \\ \beta & \text{plural} \end{bmatrix} \end{matrix}$$

indicates that the person and plurality of the verb are α and β if they are α and β for the noun-phrase, i.e., that the person and plurality of the verb are the same as those of the noun-phrase.

$$\begin{bmatrix} \alpha & \text{voc} \\ \alpha & \text{cons} \end{bmatrix}$$

indicates that a phoneme, /1/ for instance, can be said to have the features [+vocalic] and [+consonantal], if alpha is given the value $+$; if alpha is given the value $-$ the same representation will indicate that the phoneme /j/ is [$-$vocalic] and [$-$consonantal]. "We will follow the practice of using small Greek letters as variables ranging over feature specifications (that is, over the $+$ and $-$ and the integers). With this convention, we can characterize liquids and glides as the category:

$$\begin{bmatrix} \alpha & \text{vocalic} \\ \alpha & \text{consonantal} \end{bmatrix}$$ " (Chomsky and Halle 1968:83)

Other variables, X, Y, etc., representing any phrase, are also used in *structural descriptions*. Such variables indicate that an element may occur in a given position, but the rule will apply whether or not this element is null. In the sentence:

The child certainly ate the apple

the adverb *certainly* is represented by X in the structural description of this sentence for passive:

```
SD: NP  X    Aux   V    NP
     1   2    3     4    5          ⟹
SC: 5   2    3 be+en 4 by 1
```

Such a variable represents a phrase which can be null.

VERB-PHRASE (VP)

Verb-phrase is the term used to designate the *constituent* containing the verb and its complements. In *tree* representations the verb-phrase is labelled VP and it can be expanded into V NP or into V PP or V NP PP.

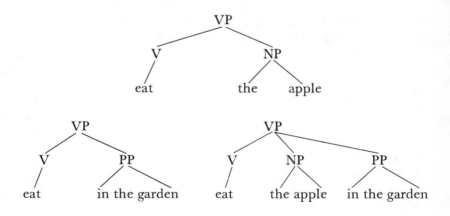

VOCALIC NUCLEUS

Within a syllable, a vowel is also called a **vocalic nucleus**. It is a simple vocalic nucleus if the vowel is simple as in *pit* p[i] t; it is a complex vocalic nucleus if the vowel is a diphthong, or considered as such, as in *fade* f[ey] d. (Chomsky and Halle, 1968:28)

W

WELL-FORMEDNESS
Well-formedness is an *intuitive* notion which involves an assessment of the *syntactic structure* and *semantic interpretation* of a sentence. (Chomsky, 1965:151)

WH—
In a *complement sentence*, a **WH-phrase** indicates either a relative clause or an interrogative sentence. "WH– words represent the relativized *constituents* in relative clauses or questioned constituents in interrogatives."

> [±WH] is a feature assigned under *COMP*
> [+WH] underlies direct or indirect questions
> [–WH] underlies relatives

(Chomsky, 1973:234-237)

WORD
A **word** is a *string* of *formatives* (one or more) between *boundaries* of the form # ... #, where ... contains no occurrence of ##. It constitutes the domain of application of the noncyclic rules of phonology. (Chomsky and Halle, 1968:13/163)

A word is a part of the *phonological representation* and, as such, it is phonologically significant. (Chomsky, 1974)

"The **terminus of a word** is any configuration of boundaries and *brackets* having the form:

$_s[\# \ X[\#$ (read: beginning of a word)
$\#]X\#]_s$ (read: end of a word)
$\#]X[\#$ (Read: end and beginning of a word)

where S is the *category* 'sentence' and X contains no segments." (Chomsky and Halle, 1968:367)

$\bar{X}$ *(X bar)*
Under the *lexicalist hypothesis*, Chomsky suggests that since the phrase *category* "complement" seems to play no role in *transformations,* it can be replaced "by a single schema, with a variable standing for the *lexical categories* N, A, V:

$$\bar{X} \rightarrow X \ldots "$$ (Chomsky, 1970a:52)

The $\bar{X}$ itself is introduced by the rule:

$$\bar{\bar{X}} \rightarrow [\text{Spec}, \bar{X}] \ \ \bar{X}$$

(read: X double bar is to be rewritten as specifer (determiner) of X bar, X bar)

BIBLIOGRAPHY

Chomsky, Noam

1956 "Three Models for the Description of Languages" in R.D. Luce, R. Bush, and E. Gallanter, eds. *Readings in Mathematical Psychology*, vol. 2, New York: Wiley, 1965.

1957 *Syntactic Structures*, The Hague: Mouton.

1959 "On Certain Formal Properties of Grammar," in Luce, Bush, Gallanter

1961a "On the Notion of Grammar" in Fodor and Katz, *The Structure of Language: Readings in the Philosophy of Language*, Englewood Cliffs, N.J.: Prentice-Hall, 1964.

1961b "Some Methodological Remarks on Generative Grammar," in *Word*, 17.

1962 "A Transformational Approach to Syntax," in Fodor & Katz. The *Structure of Language*, Prentice Hall, 1964.

1963 "Formal Properties of Grammar," in Luce, Bush, and Gallanter.

1964a "The Logical Basis of Linguistic Theory," In H. Lunt, ed. *Proceedings of the Ninth Congress of Linguistics*, Cambridge, Mass., The Hague: Mouton.

1964b "Current Issues in Linguistic Theory," in Fodor and Katz.

1965 Aspects of the Theory of Syntax, Cambridge, MIT Press.

1966a Topics in the Theory of Generative Grammar, The Hague: Mouton.

1966b Cartesian Linguistics, New York: Harper & Row.

1970a "Remarks on Nominalizaion," reprinted in *Studies on Semantics in Generative Grammar*, The Hague: Mouton, 1972.

1970b "Deep Structure, Surface Structure, and Semantic Interpretation," reprinted in *Studies on Semantics in Generative Grammar*.

1971 Problems of Knowledge and Freedom, New York: Pantheon.

1972a Language and Mind, 2nd ed., New York: Harcourt Brace Jovanovich

1972b Studies on Semantics in Generative Grammar, The Hague: Mouton.

1972c "Some Empirical Issues in the Theory of Transformational Grammar," reprinted in Chomsky 1972b.

1973 "Conditions on Transformations," in S.R. Anderson and P. Kiparsky, eds. *A Festschrift for Morris Halle*, New York: Holt, Rinehart & Winston.

1974a MIT Lectures, Spring Semester (notes)

1974b "Dialogue with Noam Chomsky," In Parret, *Discussing Language*, The Hague: Mouton.

1975a "Questions of Form and Interpretation," *Linguistic Analysis*, 1975

1975b MIT Lectures (notes)

1975c Reflections on Language, New York: Pantheon.

1975d The Logical Structure of Linguistic Theory, New York: Plenum.

Chomsky and Miller, G.A.
1958 "Finite State Language," in Luce, Bush, and Gallanter.

Chomsky and Halle, M.
1968 The Sound Pattern of English, New York: Harper and Row.

Bresnan, J.W.
1972 Theory of Complementation in English Syntax, unpublished dissertation, MIT.

Jackendoff, R.S.
1972 Semantic Interpretation in Generative Grammar, Cambridge: MIT Press.

Jacobs, J.R., and Rosenbaum, P.S.
1968 English Transformational Grammar, Waltham, Mass.: Blaisdell.

Perlmutter, D.M.
1971 Deep and Surface Structure Constraints in Syntax, New York: Holt, Rinehart & Winston.

Ross, J.R.
1967 Constraints on Variables in Syntax, unpublished dissertation, MIT.

de Saussure, F.
1966 Course in General Linguistics, New York: McGraw-Hill.

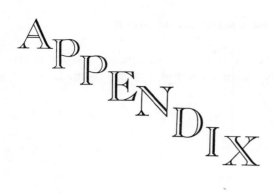

APPENDIX

The following examples of transformations will attempt to show how some of the most frequent transformations work. As in the Glossary itself, the transformations are ordered alphabetically, without reference to the formal order in which they occur.

One should keep in mind that many matters still need to be clarified about transformations. The set of all transformations is not even well defined, and there is no complete agreement among linguists on some very basic issues. Hence, the only thing we do below is to list a number of examples and give a brief bibliography.

AFFIX-HOPPING (obligatory)
In *Syntactic Structures*, Chomsky (1957) demonstrates that affixes (-s for the third person singular, zero for other persons, past, -en for past participle, -ing for present participle) introduced into the deep structure immediately before the verb,

are moved immediately to the right of the verb by a transformation subsequently called **affix-hopping** and formalized:

Af+v → v+Af

Example:

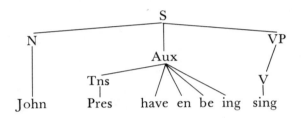

In this example the transformation does the following:

s+have → have+s which is written *has*
en +be → be+en which is written *been*
ing+sing → sing+ing which is written *singing*

The derived sentence is: John has been singing.

COMPLEMENTIZER PLACEMENT

The complementizer placement has been a much debated issue.
According to Bresnan (1970) and Chomsky (1970a and 1973),
COMP is a universal element introduced by a phrase-structure
rule S̄→ Comp S. For others, Rosenbaum (1967) the complementizer is introduced transformationally.

The transformational approach is the following: when a
complement sentence is embedded into a matrix sentence, this
transformation inserts a complementizer at the beginning of the
complement sentence. The choice of the complementizer, *that,
for-to*, or *'s-ing* is determined by the head verb. The following
sentence:

I expect that Bill will write

is derived from the underlying structure:

I expect it—Bill will write.

It gets deleted according to the *it-deletion transformation*, as soon as the COMP-placement has been applied. If there is a sequence of embedded sentences as in the sentence:

I expect that Bill wants to speak to Mary

the COMP-placement applies on each *cycle*.

The rule for COMP-placement is:

$$\text{SD: } \underset{1}{X} \; [_S \; \underset{2}{NP} \; \underset{3}{Aux} \; \underset{4}{VP} \; \underset{5}{Y}]$$

$$\text{SC: } 1 \begin{Bmatrix} \text{that} \\ \text{for—to} \\ \text{poss-ing} \end{Bmatrix} 2 \; 3 \; 4 \; 5$$

CONTRACTION (optional)

Contraction is a transformation which reduces the negative particle. The sentence:

The cat did not eat the mouse

can be transformed into:

The cat didn't eat the mouse.

The rule is formalized:

$$
\begin{array}{lccc}
& & \text{Modal} & \\
\text{SD:} & \text{Tense} & \text{Have} & \text{not} \\
& & \text{Be} & \\
& 1 & & 2 \\
\text{SC:} & 1+\text{n't} & & \phi
\end{array}
$$

DATIVE MOVEMENT (optional)

In English, the sentence "Peter gives a pen to John" has the same meaning as "Peter gives John a pen." The change which converts the first sentence into the second sentence is due to the transformation called dative movement. This transformation can only apply if the verb of the sentence is *give, lend, offer, send, build, buy, get, leave, make*. This transformation deletes the preposition *to* or *for*, and moves the NP indirect object to the left of the NP direct object, providing the latter is not a pronoun. Given the structural description of the sentence:

$$
\begin{array}{lccccc}
& \text{Peter} & \text{gives} & \text{a pen} & \text{to} & \text{John} \\
\text{SD:} & \text{NP} & \text{V} & \text{NP} & \text{to} & \text{NP} \\
& 1 & 2 & 3 & 4 & 5
\end{array}
$$

The transformation will produce the structural change:

$$
\text{SC:} \quad 1 \quad 2 \quad 5 \quad \phi \quad 3
$$

The condition is that 3 must not be a pronoun: $3=[-\text{Pro}]$

The transformation does not apply if 3 is $[+\text{Pro}]$:

> Peter gives it to him
> *Peter gives him it

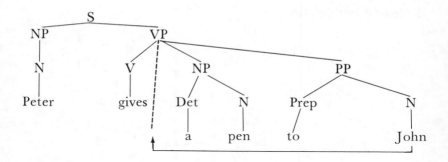

(See Fillmore: 1965, Kuroda; 1968, Jackendoff and Culi-cover: 1971.)

DELETION, AGENT (optional)
There are a number of passive sentences of the type:

> The cat was hit
> The case will be examined

where no agent is expressed. The theory is that the active corresponding sentences from which these sentences derive must be:

> Someone (or something) hit the cat
> Someone will examine the case

and not:

> *Bill (or the bicycle) hit the cat
> *The dean will examine the case.

The rule of **agent deletion** states that in a passive sentence, the agent can be deleted only if it is the indefinite pronoun, *someone* or *something*.

Rule of agent deletion:

$$SD: X - be\ en - V - Y - by\ \begin{Bmatrix} someone \\ something \end{Bmatrix}$$

$$
\begin{array}{cccccc}
 & 1 & 2 & 3 & 4 & 5 \\
SC: & 1 & 2 & 3 & 4 & \phi
\end{array}
$$

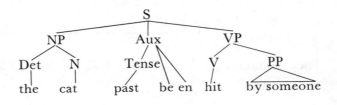

DELETION, IT (obligatory)

The **it-deletion** transformation replaces the subject NP *it* of the main verb of a sentence, by the embedded sentence which is dominated by that NP.

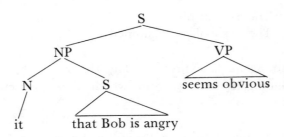

Rule of it-deletion:

$$
SD: X - \quad {}_{NP}[it - S]_{NP} - VP
$$

$$
\begin{array}{cccc}
1 & 2 & 3 & 4 \\
SC: \quad 1 & \phi & 3 & 4
\end{array}
$$

The derived sentence will be:

That Bob is angry seems obvious.

DELETION, EQUI NP (obligatory)

Equi NP deletion is the name for a *transformation* which deletes the subject of a for-to clause if it is co-referential to a *NP* (subject or object) in a higher sentence. Example:

(a) the subject of the head-sentence deletes the subject of the *embedded* sentence: "the dogs refuse to play" has the following *deep structure "the dogs* refuse—*the dogs* play."

(b) the object of the head-sentence deletes the subject of the embedded sentence: "John persuaded Mary to see the doctor" has the following *deep structure* "John persuaded *Mary—Mary* to see the doctor."

(a)

(b)

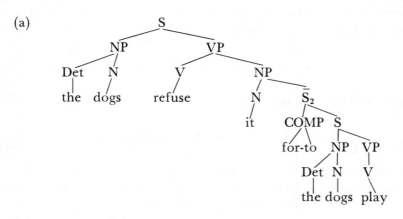

Rosenbaum (1967) proposed this transformation and Postal (1970) made substantial contributions to this subject.

The rule can be formalized:

$$\text{SD: X NP Y } [_S \left\{ \begin{array}{l} \text{for-to} \\ \text{poss-ing} \end{array} \right\} \text{NP W] Z}$$

	1	2	3		4		5	6	7	
	1	2	3		4		5	6	7	condition: 2=5
SC:	1	2	3		4		ϕ	6	7	

DELETION, GAPPING AND VP (optional)

There are a number of unsolved problems connected with deletions. Ross (1970) was the first to discuss what he called **Gapping**, that is to say, the deletion of a repeated verb in a conjoined structure. The sentence:

I ate fish, Bill ate rice, and Harry ate roast beef

can be transformed into:

I ate fish, Bill rice, and Harry roast beef.

The formulation of the rule seems easy. But in the case of more complex structures, there are several possible deletions which involve a verb, or one or several embedded clauses.

Example: I want to try to begin to write a novel, and Mary wants to try to begin to write a play.

Ross shows that several possible deletions can occur:

$$\text{Mary} \left\{ \begin{array}{l} \text{I want to try to begin to write a novel, and} \\ \text{to try to begin to write a play} \\ \text{to begin to write a play} \\ \text{to write a play} \\ \text{a play} \end{array} \right.$$

The rule cannot be expressed in terms of deletion of a constituent but of a variable. Hankamer (1973) suggests this formalization of the rule:

$$
\begin{array}{llllllllll}
\text{SD:} & \text{NP} & \text{X} & \text{A} & \text{Z} & \text{and} & \text{NP} & \text{X} & \text{B} & \text{Z} \\
 & 1 & 2 & 3 & 4 & 5 & 6 & 7 & 8 & 9 \quad \text{condition: A} \neq \text{B} \\
\text{SC:} & 1 & 2 & 3 & 4 & 5 & 6 & \phi & 8 & \phi
\end{array}
$$

Jackendoff (1971) draws a distinction between Gapping, which deletes material from the middle of a clause and **VP deletion** which deletes material from the ends of clauses. He points out that, unlike Gapping, VP deletion does not delete auxiliaries and needs do-support if tense is the only element dominated by the auxiliary node. Example:

Bob ate the peaches, and Harry did, too
Frank may have told Chet, and Joe may have, too.

Another type of variable deletion is found in comparative clauses (Hankamer 1973) as exemplified in the following sentences:

Joe likes Sue more than [Joe likes] Martha
Mary is as bright as Peter [is bright].

Finally, the deletion of a whole sentence may occur under certain circumstances and the deleted S can be replaced by *it*, by the application which Ross (1969, 1974) calls **S-Pronominalization**. "This rule operates to replace the complement objects (or subjects) of certain predicates by *it*, when these complements are identical to a sentence elsewhere in the text." (Ross 1974:71)

Bill believes that treason is pleasin', but no one else believes it is derived from:

> Bill believes that treason is pleasin', but no one else
> believes that treason is pleasin'.

DELETION, NP (optional)
In the case of conjoined sentences with identical NPs which
have identical functions and identical references, the second
occurrence of the NP can be deleted.

> Example: Birds are singing and flying

is derived from:

> Birds are singing and birds are flying.

The rule can be formalized:

$$
\begin{array}{llllllll}
\text{SD:} & \text{X NP} & \text{Y} & \text{and} & \text{Z NP} & \text{W} & \\
& 1\;\;2 & 3 & 4 & 5\;\;6 & 7 & \text{condition: } 2=6 \\
\text{SC:} & 1\;\;2 & 3 & 4 & 5\;\;\phi & 7 &
\end{array}
$$

DELETION, FOR (obligatory)
Some complement sentences are introduced by the complementizer *for-to*:

> Example: It is difficult for John to sing.

In cases where the subject of the embedded sentence has
been deleted by *Equi, for* has to be deleted in order to give the
correct sentence:

> The dogs refuse to play

derived from the underlying structure:

The dogs refuse it—for the dogs to play.

After Equi has applied, the derived structure is:

The dogs refuse for to play.

The rule of for-deletion applies when and only when *for* is adjacent to *to*. It can be formalized:

SD: X for   to   Y
     1   2   3   4
SC: 1   φ   3   4

DO-SUPPORT (obligatory)
In *Syntactic Structures*, Chomsky explains the *Affix-hopping* transformation:

Af+V → V+Af

But when an affix is not immediately followed by a verb "*do* is introduced as the 'bearer' of an unaffixed affix." (Chomsky 1957:62)

Af → do+Af

This transformation is now generally called **do-support**. It applies in questions and negations. After the Aux NP inversion has applied to a sentence whose Aux node dominates only tense, the derived structure is:

Tense NP V

In the case of negation the structure is:

Tense not V

In both cases the tense affix is said to be "stranded."

We can generalize these two cases in one structural description.

SD: X tense   Y
    1   2   3 Condition: X and Y ≠ Verb
SC: 1 do + 2 3

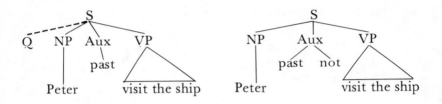

These trees represent the structures of the following two sentences:

Did Peter visit the ship?
Peter did not visit the ship.

EACH-MOVEMENT (obligatory)
This term refers to a *transformation* and its conditions of application discussed in *Conditions on Transformations*.

Example: The candidates each expected [s PRO to defeat the other]

The rule of **each-movement** applies and gives:

The candidates expected to defeat each other.

(Chomsky, 1973:238)

EXTRAPOSITION (optional)

Extraposition is a *transformation* which "detaches the *embedded* sentence from under the *domination* of the *noun phrase* of which it is a complement and moves it to the end of the main sentence." (Jacob and Rosenbaum, 1968:172) It is optional.

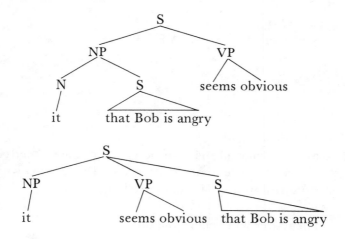

This rule applies only to a sentence which is dominated by a node NP (subject or object) which also dominates an N. Furthermore, the derivation of that N can only be the word *it*. In case the rule of extraposition does not apply, the word *it* will obligatorily be deleted by a rule called *it-deletion*.

(See Rosenbaum: 1967 and Lakoff: 1968)

IMPERATIVE (optional)

On account of a number of facts observed in sentences such as:

> Open the door, will you?
> Be on time, won't you?

it has been suggested (See Katz and Postal:1964) that the underlying structure of an imperative sentence is:

you   will   VP

The **imperative transformation** deletes the NP *you* and the Aux *will*.

$$
\begin{array}{llll}
\text{SD:} & \text{you} & \text{tense} & \text{will} & \text{VP} \\
 & 1 & 2 & 3 \\
\text{SC:} & \phi & \phi & 3
\end{array}
$$

NEGATION (obligatory)

In his article, Klima (1964) suggests that the underlying structure of a negative sentence contains a particle NEG which triggers the transformation of a sentence like:

The writer will believe the boy

into its negative counterpart:

The writer will not believe the boy.

The rule for **negation** reads:

$$
\text{SD:} \quad \text{Neg} \quad \text{NP} \quad \text{Tense} \quad \left(\left\{ \begin{array}{l} \text{Modal} \\ \text{have} \\ \text{be} \end{array} \right\} \right) \quad \text{VP}
$$

$$
\begin{array}{lllll}
 & 1 & 2 & 3 & & 4 \\
\text{SC:} & & 2 & 3+1 & & 3
\end{array}
$$

If the Auxiliary node dominates tense only as in the case of:

The writer believed the boy
(NP past   V   NP)

the negative transformation will be followed by *do-support* to generate the correct sentence:

The writer did not believe the boy.

NUMBER AGREEMENT (obligatory)
In *Syntactic Structures*, Chomsky gives the following rule:

$$C \longrightarrow \begin{cases} \text{s in the context NP sing---} \\ \phi \text{ in the context NP pl---} \\ \text{past} \end{cases}$$

(Chomsky, 1957:39)

It means that in English there are three cases of Concord (C) or **Agreement**. For the present tense the person and plurality of the verb are the same as those of the NP, affix -s for the third person singular, no affix in other cases. For the past tense all verbs receive a past affix. The rule can be expressed with *variables* in the following fashion:

$$\begin{array}{c} \text{NP} \\ \begin{bmatrix} \alpha \text{ person} \\ \beta \text{ plural} \end{bmatrix} \end{array} \quad \text{tense} \quad ===> \quad \begin{array}{c} \text{NP} \\ \begin{bmatrix} \alpha \text{ person} \\ \beta \text{ plural} \end{bmatrix} \end{array} \quad \text{tense}$$

PARTICLE MOVEMENT
The relationship between the two following sentences:

    a) Peter called up his friend
    b) Peter called his friend up

can be captured by a rule which shows how sentence (a) can be optionally transformed into (b).
    Particle movement rule:

SD: NP V Part. NP
      1   2   3   4
SC: 1   2   4   3

But when the NP object is a pronoun the rule is obligatory:

*Peter called up him
Peter called him up.

This fact must be stated in the rule.

PASSIVE TRANSFORMATION (optional)

The **passive transformation** replaces a sentence such as:

The cat ate the mouse

by:

The mouse was eaten by the cat.

The transformation moves the NP object to the position of the NP subject; and the NP subject is moved to the right of the VP and preceded by the particle *by*. The auxiliary be+en is added to the existing Aux node. The structural description of the sentence in order that the rule apply is:

SD: NP Aux V NP
      1   2 3 4

The effect produced by the structural change is:

SC: 4   2 be+en 3 by 1

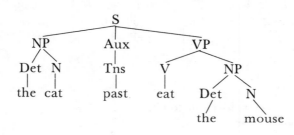

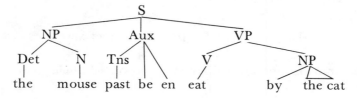

There are a number of problems about this transformation:

(a) How is the particle *by* inserted? Here Chomsky's method has been adopted. (Chomsky 1957:43 and 1965:104-105)
(b)What verbs cannot be submitted to passive transformation? Such verbs as *resemble, have,* etc., do not have passive transformation.
(c) Is it true that there is no difference in meaning between the active and passive sentences?

PRONOMINALIZATION (obligatory)
In their article "Rules for English Pronominalization," Lees and Klima (1963) propose the pronoun rule:

"X — Nom — Y — Nom´ $\longrightarrow$ X — Nom — Y — Nom´ + Pro — Z

where Nom = Nom´, and where Nom is in a matrix sentence while Nom´ is in a constituent sentence embedded within that matrix sentence."
    In the more usual notation the rule reads:

$$\text{SD:} \quad \text{X NP} \quad \text{Y} \; [_S \quad \text{Z NP} \quad \text{W}]$$

SD: X NP   Y [$_S$ Z NP   W]
     1 2   3   4 5   6   Condition 2=5
SC: 1 2   3   4 5   6
                       [+Pro]

In the example:

> Mary told John to protect her

the underlying structure is:

> Mary told John for John to protect Mary.

Pronominalization takes place in the lower sentence giving:

> for John to protect her

Then the subject of the lower sentence is deleted by *Equi NP deletion.*

   (For further discussion of the subject see Postal: 1970 and Lakoff: 1970.)

QUESTION TRANSFORMATION (obligatory)
There are two types of questions:

(a) the interrogation by inversion whose answer is yes/no:

> Will Peter visit the ship?

(b) the interrogation beginning with an interrogative particle and whose answer is a phrase:

> What will Peter visit?

   According to Katz and Postal (1964), the deep structure contains an element Q (for Question) which triggers the inversion of the NP subject and the auxiliary:

SD: Q NP   tense ($\begin{Bmatrix} \text{Modal} \\ \text{have} \\ \text{be} \end{Bmatrix}$) V NP

$\qquad$ 1 2 $\qquad\qquad$ 3 $\qquad\qquad$ 4 5

SC: $\qquad$ 3 $\qquad\qquad$ 2 $\qquad\qquad$ 4 5

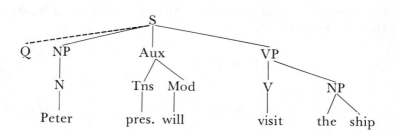

In sentences like:

Peter visited the ship

where the Aux node only dominates tense, the Question transformation introduces another transformation called *do-support* to generate the correct sentence:

Did Peter visit the ship?

In the second type of question:

What will Peter visit?

besides the element Q there is also an element +WH dominated by the NP node which is being queried. In this case the inversion transformation performed in the first case is preceded by the fronting of the WH morpheme. This transformation takes place in two stages:

(i)   WH-fronting, or WH-movement:

SD: Q   NP   Aux   V   NP
                                    +WH
          1   2   3   4   5
SC: 1 5 2   3   4   φ

(ii) Aux NP inversion applies to the derived structure and gives the correct sentence:

What will Peter visit?

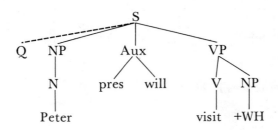

WH-movement is a widely discussed problem and there are diverging views:

(a) Jackendoff (1969) and Chomsky (1973) claim that Wh-movement is a *cyclic rule* and a sentence like:

Whom did they believe that Mary said that John saw?

must have the following underlying structure:

$$\Big[\text{COMP they believe} \Big[\text{COMP Mary said [COMP John saw + WH]} \Big] \Big]$$

On each cycle the Wh-word moves to the head of the sentence until it reaches the matrix sentence.

(b) Bach (1971a) and Postal (1972) claim that WH-movement is a *last cyclic rule.*

RAISING (obligatory)

Raising, a term coined by Kiparsky (1970), defines a *transformation* which moves an element from an *embedded* sentence into a higher position. It is a controversial subject because some linguists (Postal: 1974, Szamosi: 1973 and others) argue that there are two rules of Raising: Raising to object position with verbs like *believe* and Raising to subject position with verbs like *seem,* while Chomsky (1973) recognizes only the rule of Raising to subject position.

(a) Raising to subject position: the subject of the embedded sentence becomes the subject of the main predicate.

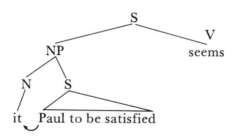

(b) Raising to object position: the subject of the embedded sentence becomes the object of the main predicate.

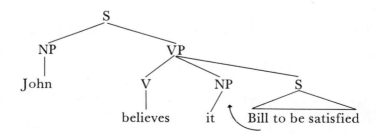

This has been a much debated issue and there is a great deal of literature on the subject: Rosenbaum (1967), Lakoff (1968), Kiparsky and Kiparsky (1970), McCawley (1970), Chomsky (1973), Szamosi (1973), Berman (1974).

REFLEXIVIZATION (obligatory)

In their article "Rules for English Pronominalization," Lees and Klima (1963) propose the reflexive rule:

"$X - Nom - Y - Nom' - Z \longrightarrow X - Nom - Y - Nom' + Self - Z$

where Nom=Nom' = a nominal and where Nom and Nom' are within the same simplex sentence."

In the more usual notation the rule reads:

	X	NP	Y	NP	Z	
SD:	1	2	3	4	5	Condition 2=4
SC:	1	2	3	4	5	
			[+Refl]			

In the example:

Mary told John to protect himself

the underlying structure is:

Mary told John for John to protect John.

Reflexivization takes place in the lower sentence giving:

for John to protect himself.

Then the NP subject of the lower sentence is deleted by *Equi NP deletion*.

RELATIVIZATION (obligatory)

Relativization is the transformation which embeds a sentence into the NP of another sentence, providing that NP is identical to one of the NP in the embedded sentence. The sentence:

The boy (that) I saw was reading the paper

is transformationally derived from the following underlying structure:

The boy [$_S$ I saw the boy] was reading the paper.

The relativized NP is replaced by WH which is moved to the beginning of the embedded sentence.

The rule can be formalized:

$$
\begin{array}{llllllll}
\text{SD: W} & \text{NP} & [_S & \text{X NP} & \text{Y]} & \text{Z} & \\
1 & 2 & & 3 \quad 4 & 5 & 6 & \text{Condition: 2=4} \\
\text{SC: 1} & 2 & 4 & 3 \quad \phi & 5 & 6 & \\
& & [\text{WH}] & & & &
\end{array}
$$

There is disagreement among the linguists on how to analyze the relative clauses. It has been suggested that relative clauses are derived from conjoined sentences (Thompson: 1971). The most generally accepted analysis, namely that NP dominates S, is subdivided into two alternatives: (a) S is immediately dominated by the Determiner node of the NP (Chomsky: 1965); and (b) S is dominated by the NP node (Ross: 1967).

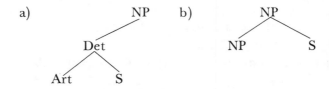

TAG FORMATION (optional)

> The cat will eat the mouse, won't he?
> You can open the window, can't you?
> Mary has not read the paper, has she?
> You sing, don't you?

This type of question following a statement is called a tag. The **tag transformation** consists in repeating the original sentence and (a) adding to it the first auxiliary followed by *n't*, in case the main verb is affirmative, or (b) adding the first auxiliary without *n't*, in case the main verb is negative, and in both cases repeating the pronominalized NP subject of the main verb. The rule can be formalized:

$$
\text{SD: Q} \quad \text{(not)} \quad \text{NP} \quad \text{Tense} \quad \left(\begin{Bmatrix} \text{Modal} \\ \text{Have} \\ \text{Be} \end{Bmatrix} \right) \text{X}
$$

$$
\begin{array}{cccccc}
 & 1 & 2 & 3 & 4 & 5 \\
\text{SC:} & & 2 & 3 & 4 & 5\ 4\ 3 \\
 & & & & & [\text{Pro}]
\end{array}
$$

THAT-INSERTION (obligatory)

That-insertion refers to the transformation which requires that *COMP* be replaced by *that* after certain verbs and when the verb is tensed:

> I expected (that) you would be there

but not:

> *I expected that to be there

where the verb is infinitive (not tensed). (See Chomsky 1973:244ff.)

Later on, *that* is optionally deleted.

THERE-INSERTION *(optional)*

The transformation called there-insertion changes the sentence:

> A dog is in the garden

into:

> There is a dog in the garden.

This transformation is limited to sentences with the verb *to be* and a small class of intransitive verbs (*appear, rise, come,* etc.). It moves the NP subject to the right of the verb and inserts *there* as the surface subject of the sentence. The NP subject of the kernel sentence must be indefinite. The rule can be formalized:

SD:	NP	be	
	[–def]		
	1	2	
SC:	there	2	1

There are a number of unsolved problems associated with this rule. See Lakoff (1972) for counterexamples.

TOPICALIZATION *(optional)*

Topicalization is a transformation which consists in preposing a NP over a *variable* in order to focus attention on that NP.

> Example: This book you should read

is derived from:

> You should read this book.

The rule reads:

$$
\begin{array}{llll}
\text{SD:} & \text{X} & \text{NP} & \text{Y} \\
 & 1 & 2 & 3 \\
\text{SC:} & 2 \ 1 & \phi & 3
\end{array}
$$

(For discussion, see Ross 1967:115ff.)

WH-MOVEMENT

WH-movement is a general term which refers to two transformations:

(a)   *question transformation*

(b)   *relative clause transformation.*

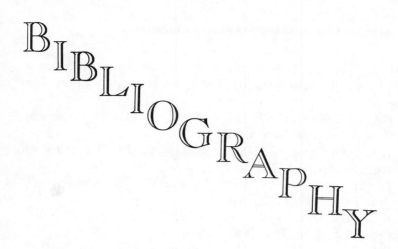

BIBLIOGRAPHY

E. Bach (1971a). "Questions", *Linguistic Inquiry,* 2: 153-166.

A. Berman (1974). "On the VSO Hypothesis", Linguistic Inquiry, 5:1-37

J. Bresnan (1970). "On Complementizers: Toward a Syntactic Theory of Complement Types", *Foundation of Language,* 6:297-321

N. Chomsky (1957). *Syntactic Structures,* Mouton, The Hague

N. Chomsky (1965). *Aspects of the Theory of Syntax,* MIT Press, Cambridge

N. Chomsky (1970a). "Remarks on Nominalization," reprinted in *Studies on Semantics in Generative Grammar,* The Hague, Mouton, 1972

N. Chomsky (1973). "Conditions on Transformations" in S.R. Anderson and P. Kiparsky, eds. *A Festschrift for Morris Halle,* New York

Emonds, J. (1970). *Root and Structure-Preserving Transformations,* unpublished Doctoral dissertation, Massachusetts Institute of Technology.

C.J. Fillmore (1965). *Indirect Object Constructions in English and the Ordering of Transformations*, Mouton, The Hague

C.J. Fillmore and D.T. Langendoen, eds. (1971). *Studies in Linguistic Semantics*, New York

J.A. Fodor and J.J. Katz, eds. (1964). *The Structure of Language*, Englewood Cliffs

J. Hankamer (1973). "Unacceptable Ambiguity", *Linguistic Inquiry*, 4:17-68

R.S. Jackendoff (1969). *Some Rules of Semantic Interpretation for English*, PhD Dissertation, MIT

R.S. Jackendoff (1971). "Gapping and Related Rules," *Linguistic Inquiry*, 2:21-35

R. S. Jackendoff and P.W. Culicover. (1971) "A Reconsideration of Dative Movement", *Foundation of Language*, 7:397-412

R.A. Jacobs and P.S. Rosenbaum (1968). *English Transformational Grammar*, Waltham, Mass.

J.J. Katz and P.M. Postal (1964). *An Integrated Theory of Linguistic Descriptions*,   MIT Press

R.P. Kiparsky and C. Kiparsky (1970). "Fact" in M. Bierwisch and K. Heidolph, eds. *Progress in Linguistics*, The Hague

E.S. Klima (1964). "Negation in English" in Fodor and Katz

Koutsoudas, A. (1972). "The Strict Order Fallacy," *Language* 48:88-96

Koutsoudas, A. (1973). "Extrinsic Order and the Complex NP Constraint," *Linguistic Inquiry* 4:69-81

S.Y. Kuroda (1968). "Review of Fillmore (1965)", *Language*, 44:374-378

G. Lakoff (1968b). *Deep and Surface Grammar*, mimeographed, Indiana Linguistic Club

G. Lakoff (1970a). *Irregularity in Syntax,* New York

G. Lakoff (1972). *Where the Rules Fail*, mimeographed, Indiana Linguistics Club

R.B. Lees and E.S. Klima (1963). "Rules for English Pronominalization", *Language*, 39:17-28

Lehman, T. (1972). "Some Arguments Against Ordered Rules," *Language* 48:541-550.

J. McCawley (1970). "English as a VSO Language", *Language*, 46:286-299

P.M. Postal (1970b). "On Coreferential Complement Subject Deletion" *Linguistic Inquiry*, 1:439-500

P.M. Postal (1972). "On Some Rules that are not Successive Cyclic" *Linguistic Inquiry*, 3:211-222

P.M. Postal (1974). *On Raising,* MIT Press

D.A. Reibel and S.A. Schane, eds. (1969). *Modern Studies in English*, Prentice Hall

Ringen, C. (1972). "On Arguments for Rule Ordering," *Foundations of Language* 8:266-273.

P.S. Rosenbaum, (1967). *The Grammar of English Predicate Complement Constructions*, MIT Press

J.R. Ross (1967). *Constraints on Variables in Syntax*, PhD Dissertation, MIT

J.R. Ross (1969). "Adjectives as Noun Phrases" in Reibel and Schane, eds.

J.R. Ross (1970). "Gapping and the Order of Constituents" in M. Bierwisch and K. Heidolph, eds. *Progress in Linguistics*, Mouton, The Hague

J.R. Ross (1974). "Three Batons for Cognitive Psychology" in W.B. Weimer and D.S. Palermo, eds. *Cognition and the Symbolic Processes,* 63-124

M. Szamosi (1973). "On the Unity of Subject Raising" in C. Corum, T. Smith-Stark, and A Weiser, eds. *Papers from the Ninth Regional Meeting of the Chicago Linguistic Society*

S.A. Thompson (1971). "The Deep Structure of Relative Clauses" in C.J. Fillmore and D.T. Langendoen

The Situation of Linguistics
Joseph F. Graham
State University of New York at Binghamton

A new science brings new hope, and that hope expands with early success to encourage continuing growth. In reverse, failure can be discouraging to the point of despair. Hopes went very high with the rise of linguistics, though not without reason. Here at last was a science of language which seemed to promise so much, to the very extent that language itself reached so far in so many directions. There was soon a mass of problems in line for solution, with some eagerly expecting what could only be a miracle and others impatient for having to wait at all. It should have been obvious that under such badly strained conditions some disappointment was inevitable. The linguists have not been able to solve every problem for everyone; they have not yet solved many of their own.

There has indeed been a reaction with a certain amount of resentment against the often excessive claims made in the name of linguistics, then so proudly represented by common metaphor as a pilot science. The real opposition must be ascribed to a basic difference in epistemology which determines the nature of scientific knowledge, its method and object, its rigors as well as its limits, and thus its possible use in the study of language. Now the difficult question is how to know whether there ever would be a true science of language, especially since the recent history of linguistics has been interpreted to deny that possibility. These allegations are serious, in that they proceed by inference from local failure in application to a general fault in the very conception of linguistic science. The complaint is already familiar, being always the same: something has been left out. But this is really an argument that no theory will ever grasp language in all of its manifestations, as if any one theory even should do just that.

Linguistics was founded on the premise that language, in its entirety and integrity, could not be understood without first restricting the field. Many critics, who operate with an ideological concept of science as absolute knowledge suddenly springing forth in full growth and strength and who ordinarily invoke the facts of a case, have little sense of the actual history of science in its factual development. They have no more respect for the limits of learning. You either know all or know nothing, they would seem to think. Science requires much more patience and moderation in working towards a knowledge of something specific. And to learn this lesson of learning is to understand the situation of knowledge along with its special strategy. This is the real reason to follow the historical development of a science like linguistics, for only then is the example to be finally appreciated and to be just as fully exploited, for only then is the true model of linguistics accurately presented because appropriately situated in the history of scientific thought.

The rise of modern linguistics is subject to interpretation according to various definitions of object and method, which always involve judgments of history as well as theory.[1] In purely analytical terms, a modern science of language became feasible once language was finally recognized as an independent and coherent body of phenomena worthy of study. In more empirical terms, several trends and moments have been important contributions to the present state of linguistics. The development of comparative philology during the nineteenth century provided evidence for the relations among the Indo-

European languages and the means to trace their evolution. The study of language took a different direction, away from causal explanations which proved to be generally inadequate for the broad definition of language itself and particularly impractical for the close description of languages in themselves. An idea of structure was elaborated to analyze language into functional relations for these specific conditions. And it was this structural linguistics, though in diverse forms, which came to dominate both the historical and the theoretical study of language during the first half of the twentieth century.

The original foundation for a science of language was firmly established by Ferdinand de Saussure in his *Cours de linguistique générale* of 1916 which is now widely celebrated as an inaugural date in the history of linguistics.[2] From the very beginning, Saussure attempted to distinguish clearly what is the proper object of linguistics from what is the broad subject of language. There are three initial and essential terms: *le langage* (human speech); *la langue* (language); *la parole* (speaking). The first includes the other two and represents the subject matter of linguistics, language in all of its manifestations. As part of this whole, language (in what is now the strict and technical sense of *la langue*) is designated as the object of linguistics in distinction and abstraction from speaking, *la parole*. The former is a social unity, a general system of communication shared by a community; the latter is an individual activity, an act of communication made by a specific person. The relations between language and speaking are naturally reciprocal, the one being necessary for comprehension, the other for constitution; but they are essentially different. Language is something potential and fixed like a code; speaking is something actual and variable like a message.

Language is then described as a system of signs in which the structure determines the elements, and not *vice versa* as would be the case with units of definite or separate substance, like labels attached to items. The elements of language, e.g., specific sounds, forms, or words, simply cannot be separated from the system of language, because the only elements in the system are the functions and relations established by the system. And this is the principle of structure in language, the major discovery of linguistics and the basic principle of all signification. As in every other form of signification, it is the system which determines the signs, not just regulating but actually constituting the signs as signs of that system. It is the system which makes the difference and thus establishes the distinction. Saussure compares language to the game of chess, which is a formal set of rules and not a special array of pieces, nor any sequence of moves, nor even a series of games. By analogy, language is not to be confounded with a stock of words, a sample of sentences, or even the sum total of human speech.

The principle of structure in language coincides with the principle of science for linguistics. Saussure maintains quite consistently that the relevant features of a language are never given as such but rather discovered in their mutual relations as the elements of an entire system. The identification of an element therefore supposes the recognition of a system, just as the function of an element requires the articulation of a system. And Saussure finally argues that the linguistic sign is both arbitrary and differential, being essentially relative like any conventional form and thus to be identified only in and with a set of relations which coordinate its position within the system.

With its rejection of any theory to first ascertain the facts, radical empiricism may be seen to represent the very negation rather than the real condition of a science for language. Without some explicit sense of pertinence, the so-called facts of language have no theoretical importance whatsoever; they prove nothing and only imply some arbitrary selection which they are usually thought to deny. Such a naive standard of evidence cannot possibly solve the initial problem of theory, where the issue is not the conclusion to be drawn from evidence but the constitution to be made of evidence, simply because the validity of the standard requires the resolution of the problem. In direct opposition to empiricism, the conception of structure in language (*la langue*) as the proper object of linguistics is meant to solve this theoretical problem by providing a necessary and sufficient definition of the specific difference in language and to thus determine the basic fact of language as such—the very fact that it is language and not something else.

The year 1957 marks another major event in the history of linguistics with the publication of *Syntactic Structures* by Noam Chomsky, whose work came largely in reaction to the then dominant trend of structuralism in the study of language as it had developed from Saussure and other Europeans to triumph in the United States under the broad influence of Leonard Bloomfield.[3] Whereas Saussure is now generally recognized as the founder of modern linguistics, Chomsky is still considered by many a revolutionary and even feared by some as a threat to the academic if not the scientific status of their discipline. There was a struggle, both political and intellectual, during those first ten years, when the basic theory of transformational generative grammar was being elaborated and then promoted by Chomsky and others usually associated in some way with M.I.T. The situation has changed almost as dramatically in the last ten years with much new work challenging as dogma what was heresy not long ago; but most would now agree that the original turn away from American structuralism did effectively constitute a break in the history of linguistics. And it has become common to refer to that event as a revolution, the Chomskyan Revolution.

Exactly what is meant by a revolution in the history of science has recently become a matter of controversy in itself, but the general sense does suggest something like a radical change in the orientation of a science. The crucial idea is that ordinary, everyday science has to operate for efficiency within the limits of an established order, or paradigm,[4] which combines in a solution the actual elimination of those fundamental, mostly theoretical problems necessarily neglected in the practical business of the laboratory. Only now and then, when something goes wrong, does the paradigm ever come to be suspected in itself, eventually rejected and replaced. Such a shift in paradigm does then effect a dramatic turn in the history of that science, clearly a revolution, which means progress to its proponents but catastrophe to its opponents.

To understand the revolutionary significance of transformational generative grammar in these terms, it must be compared directly with the earlier structural linguistics so as to determine the radical or essential difference between the two paradigms—that of Saussure and that of Chomsky. Certain precautions are strongly recommended if not actually required. Any characterization of either structural linguistics or transformational generative grammar involves some degree of generalization, because of the diversity in the former and the continuing development in the latter. Any comparison of these two competitive paradigms should be fully rigorous but hardly neutral, especially since the current definition of linguistic science lies at stake. The discussion has always been serious and the debate sometimes acrimonious. Many would argue that the issue has yet to be finally decided.

There are several points of comparison which would yield various differences between the structural paradigm of Saussure and the generative paradigm of Chomsky; but the general point of comparison could well be lost in the process, like comparing apples and oranges. It could be shown, that the two were different in emphasis placed on phonology as against syntax, or pattern as against rule. But it could also be shown that the two paradigms were different in success at certain universities rather than others, or with one age group rather than another. As simple, brute facts, any set of differences may be either true or false, but as evidence for a comparison, they must be judged for their relevance to the very basis of comparison, whether it be linguistics or some other study.

Both similarity and difference are necessarily relative, and no two things could ever be similar or different in any absolute sense. Two paradigms are significantly different only if they are also significantly similar, at least when they belong to the same science. Chomsky works within linguistics, as Saussure once did, however differently. That science of language, that same enterprise to which they are both supposed to belong, actually has to be defined, for one of the principal differences between the two paradigms does involve just that definition. The general terms are almost the same. In both conceptions, the linguist has to specify his own object and to proceed with his own method of study. Language, in the strict sense, is a construct of science which does correspond to something real but not necessarily to something obviously manifest because it is essentially more abstract than any sound, word, or utterance. Saussure and Chomsky share the fundamental conviction that science has to be theoretically explicit so as to be empirically accurate, but in their particular applications of this common program, the results are quite different. In retrospect, it could be said that Chomsky fulfills the promise first made and yet also broken by Saussure—the very promise to preserve linguistics from empiricism. The relation between the two will have to be described in terms more complex than simple opposition or identity, and with specific reference to their efforts against the errors of empiricism.

Within the paradigm of transformational generative grammar, natural languages are first represented as formal systems similar to those systems already known from the study of mathematical logic. A language is defined as a set of sentences, and a sentence is defined as a string or sequence of elements drawn from a definite vocabulary. These initial definitions apply to any and every language, whether natural or artificial, familiar or exotic; and they are indeed general enough, so that English may be defined as the set of English sentences without any distortion but with no more information. Some further definition is required to specify that particular set of sentences. Such specification is provided by a theory of the language, serving to identify all and only those sentences which are properly English. The task is not trivial, nor is it empirical in the ordinary sense; for the set of English sentences does not include every string of English elements, many of which are not any sentence at all, and yet it does include more than have ever been spoken or heard. A sentence seems obvious, but only in utterance; and this is to say that a sentence is not simply an utterance. The one is abstract, the other concrete; they are neither identical nor equivalent and are not to be confused. The same sentence may be uttered more than once, and some sentences have never been uttered.

A generative grammar is a specific theory of sentences; it is not a theory of utterances, even though its evidence comes from utterances. And yet it may well be asked what or even where are these strange sentences, especially those which have never been perceived. Just how are they to be conceived, when they have no place in a purely structural, strictly empirical theory of language? Sentences were not included in the study of language by Saussure, who drew the line between *langue* and *parole* so as to exclude them, never imagining that any sentence could be bound by linguistic rule, except for certain fixed expressions. His idea of structure in language was later applied to the construction of sentences by those American structuralists who immediately preceded Chomsky in the study of syntax. And Chomsky's criticism was directed against their dogmatic empiricism, which made them abstain from theory in the name of science. Their hope was to discover the rules of syntax by simple induction from a sample of utterances. This restriction to observed data was thought to guarantee objectivity, when it arbitrarily reduced the form of its object to patterns of distribution and the function of its method to segmentation and classification, corresponding to the only principles of structure for Saussure: the paradigmatic relation of contrast and the syntagmatic relation of context. The result was to preclude from linguistics an understanding of what every speaker of any language clearly knows--the grammar of that language.

Knowledge of a language, the knowledge demonstrated by every fluent speaker-hearer of that language, may be thought to function like a theory of language, one which specifies or generates, in this technical sense, the set of grammatically well-formed strings of the language, and it may also be thought to constitute an internal, mental grammar for the very same reason. On this claim of equivalence, a generative grammar should fully represent in theoretical terms that specific knowledge, or linguistic competence, most readily interpreted as a faculty of the human mind which determines external behavior or verbal performance, though not completely or directly, since the relation of system to use is mediated by other, nonlinguistic factors—all those physical, psychological, and social factors which further determine our actual speaking. The task of the linguist is then to match two types of knowledge represented by two types of grammar, the one theoretical and explicit, the other psychological and implicit. To do so, he must still abstract from the incidents of performance only those traits relevant to competence, but in so doing he may well consult for example his own or any other knowledge of language, since the purpose of linguistics is now to provide a general theory of that very knowledge which both precedes and exceeds any available evidence. The theoretical mode of representation, the explicit grammar for that knowledge has to be broadly projective or predictive, rather than narrowly descriptive, because the number of sentences of any human language are potentially infinite.

Knowledge of English is accordingly a knowledge of those sentences which are properly English, as against those which are not, because either they are French or Japanese, or simply not English. Such knowledge does not guarantee that behavior will follow exactly; it may differ in various ways both intentionally and accidentally. We know sentences, but we speak utterances, and there is a world between the two. The difference between competence and performance is not a discrepancy, however, nothing like a fault to be corrected in the manner of traditional pedagogy, for the rules of generative grammar are not prescriptions but explanations. They are not meant to dictate how we should speak, but rather to indicate something about how we can speak the way we do. The explanation is only partial, to the very extent that grammar is only part of speaking. The linguistic competence represented by a generative grammar does explain our ability to recognize and to produce new and different sentences, including those never heard or spoken before, by virtue of rules which specify all the possible sentences to be derived within a given language. Such is the ability of every speaker-hearer whose knowledge is not just a list of past utterances to be recognized and merely reproduced but a system of rules implied by—though not limited to the evidence of—any verbal behavior, no matter how rich and complex. And an adequate theory of language has then to be generative in this way; it has to represent the basic fact that human language operates with the capacity to generate an infinite, and yet very definite, set of sentences. But it has to do much more.

Knowledge of a language surely implies more than just an ability to tell the difference between grammatical and ungrammatical sequences. And what we know about the form of sentences in English does run much deeper and wider, while providing the necessary information for our judgments about the right and wrong formation of sentences. After all, we even know different degrees of ungrammaticalness, the now familiar difference between (1) and (2), taking the first examples from *Syntactic Structures*.

(1) Colorless green ideas sleep furiously.
(2) Furiously sleep ideas green colorless.

We also know the difference between two possible readings for one and the same sequence (3), where the order of the elements is not sufficient to determine their relations unambiguously.

3) old men and women
   (a) old (men and women)
   (b) (old men) and women

Another classic example of ambiguity (4) serves to illustrate a common expression in English, the X-ing of the NP, where the noun phrase may be either the subject or the object of the action.

(4) The shooting of the hunters was atrocious.

In actual utterance, these expressions are easily understood, one way or the other, because they are further determined by features of context. But the point is rather that our knowledge of language does include the ability to associate form with meaning even when the relation is neither direct nor consistent, even when it is not apparent. These simple cases, and many more complex, show that we are somehow able to assign different structures to superficially identical sentences, just as we assign identical structures to different sentences, when we recognize the relations between active and passive, positive and negative, affirmative and interrogative versions of a given expression.

A complete theory of linguistic competence will then have to provide, along with the means to distinguish the grammatical from the ungrammatical, some further means to describe the structure of sentences and the structural relations among sentences, since we know them as well. It was Chomsky who first proposed this full task for grammar and then proved that no previous attempt could have ever succeeded for want of the right techniques. Even when set to work and thus made generative, the best form of structural grammar would fail. It was not adequate, because it was not transformational. The basic principles of structural analysis, those of similarity and contiguity, were simply too weak, being limited to a single level of phrase structure. The only way to represent all the features of syntax was to introduce a special and more powerful type of rule which would relate two different phrase structures. These transformations would provide full structural descriptions in the form of a derivation including an initial deep structure and a final surface structure. With this formal innovation, it was possible to explain how a single surface structure could be derived from two different deep structures so as to produce an ambiguity. It also became possible to explain other series of phenomena, such as inversion and deletion, all out of range for simple phrase structure grammars, which could be generative but not transformational.

The combined effect of these two requirements—that a truly adequate grammar be both transformational and generative—has been to separate the theory from the evidence in both scope and depth; for the theory has to exceed the evidence in two directions, going beyond the most complete and most accurate sample of utterances to predict other sentences and to posit other structures. But in this projection of theory beyond evidence, transformational generative grammar is no exception to the rule of science, where rigor is gained not lost by generality and abstraction, for every scientific theory is not completely determined by empirical evidence. And yet what should be considered as strength has always been attacked as weakness in the theory. Almost all the objections, whether local and technical or general and philosophical, are actually directed against that necessarily inaugural distinction between competence and performance which identifies the proper object of linguistics—its real object of knowledge and in that sense its empirical object—as some property or faculty of the human mind, admittedly something not yet clearly defined. Some contend that nothing so abstract could ever be verified or even falsified, while others just complain that no such object is known to exist. These contentions beg the same question about the exact relation between theory and evidence required for scientific knowledge.

Within the structuralist paradigm, linguistic theory could be elaborated in direct relation to the evidence, and the very idea of structure as simple substitution and correlation could easily be attributed to the actual, even physical arrangement of some organized whole, the body of evidence in the literal sense of corpus. Even though Saussure insisted on the need to distinguish language as system from language as phenomena, he could only conceive that system in phenomenal terms, in terms of its empirical manifestation, and thus in terms of what he could readily perceive. The entire structuralist program was limited by that model of language as an inventory of signs, a system of elements rather than rules, a model that could only represent part of language. The rest was beyond the conceptual reach of the structuralists, especially the Americans, who refused to consider the evidence in their own knowledge of language which extended farther and deeper than what they were willing to admit in science, simply because their idea of science was so restricted. They were caught in their own prejudice against what they disparaged as mentalism, the illegitimate recourse to abstract, ideal or mental objects in any scientific explanation. This prejudice about the nature of science first prevented them from realizing that language as such is nowhere available in any integral form (unless it be found in the human brain, to which not even the most adamant empiricists have demanded access) and then from recognizing that any study of language limited to or by what is directly available could never be more than partial.

The same conditions for the study of language prevail within the transformational generative paradigm. Language is not open to immediate observation or complete examination. These conditions are commonly accepted in more sophisticated fields like nuclear physics: few are bothered by the fact that elementary particles are invisible to the human eye or that they seem to behave in strangely erratic ways. And yet the ordinary idea of science is bound to more solid ground, those fields of rather primitive taxonomy still close to natural history. Structural linguistics was not very different from these in method and object, gathering and gleaning another precious array of facts. The very purpose and the great achievement of the Chomskyan revolution was to demonstrate that linguistics not only should but actually could do more than just arrange the evidence of human speech. But it was first necessary to review and eventually to revise the very program of the discipline, which did not promote the discovery of new facts so much as would a radically new interpretation for the old facts and a recovery of those long neglected facts in our intuition of grammatical form, our own sense for language, which led into linguistic competence much like a royal road. Finally with the use of techniques developed in the study of formal systems, it became possible to imagine what a head we must have for language. That prospect alone was fascinating: at last a look into the mind! But caution was advised for this type of speculation which has always been controversial. Linguistics is hardly a neutral subject like physics, which tends to leave most heads cool or indifferent.

Much of the recent controversy has been philosophical: a rather dramatic confrontation between an old, established empiricism and the new rationalism. Many linguists also resist this trend in the revolution, regarding it as an unfortunate reversion to an earlier stage when linguistics was merely a branch of psychology and when specific differences among natural languages were overlooked in the search for some universal grammar common to all because it was close to the very laws of human thought. Bloomfield had argued that linguistics could become a rigorous and autonomous science only in direct opposition to the idea of general grammar, whereas Chomsky has expressed great sympathy for the search for a universal grammar. He has made the affinity quite explicit in writing about the classical tradition of European rationalism, notably in his *Cartesian Linguistics* of 1966, where he proposes a serious revaluation of earlier attempts to reconstruct that capacity of mind operating in language. Though he defends the independence of grammar from logic, against the tendency in some versions of rationalism to derive the one from the other, and though he now speaks of language as a "mental organ," one clearly coordinated with and yet distinct from others, Chomsky does consider the only significance of that specific difference to be the contribution of linguistics to the field of cognitive psychology, where it surely belongs. Indeed, he sees no other way to make sense of transformational generative grammar.

The argument follows from a parallel already drawn between two types of knowledge and two types of grammar representing that knowledge. It was first established that the principles of human language could not be attributed only to the regular order of data according to the structuralist model of items in arrangement; they were simply too complex. And thus the need for transformations in the study of syntax not only introduced a new model—one of items in process—but also forced a different interpretation on the entire project. Such abstract structures and relations did not appear at the one level of evidence duly recognized by the structuralists. And the whole point of transformational analysis was to describe those features of syntax which lay below that surface level and which had to be explained in other than empirical terms. But prior to any explanation, those deep structures had to be discovered, and that very discovery had to be explained or somehow justified, lest it seem quite arbitrary and capricious—as indeed it must seem to most empiricists. One explanation will serve in both cases, for the recognition of these abstract principles of grammar has to be attributed to our knowledge of language, the same knowledge consulted by the linguist through intuition about grammatical relations and the very knowledge then represented by transformational generative grammar in explicit, systematic form. But this explanation would not go far enough, were it to leave that knowledge still to be explained. If we only say that we know the language, we could well be asked exactly how we do know it or how we ever learn it, especially without our offering empirical evidence.

These last two questions have the same or almost the same answer for one very important reason: there is a close analogy between problems of method and problems of learning, those of the linguist constructing a theory and those of a child acquiring a language. The rationalist admits that if we could conceive only what we first perceive directly, then we could never learn the language we know, simply because that language contains more in depth and scope than we could ever receive through the senses. And yet we do know it. There is no paradox in such knowledge beyond perception, no mystery in learning, unless we assume that the mind begins with little or nothing of its own. The empiricist makes that assumption which the rationalist tries to refute. Chomsky argues that no linguist, no more than any child, could learn the structure of a language from the evidence of his senses, without some initial hypothesis to guide his choice of an appropriate theory or grammar, again because this evidence alone would not support any firm conclusion. The necessary hypothesis is provided by the principles of universal grammar, which define and thus delimit the class of possible languages, among which it is then feasible to choose the right one according to the available evidence. The child learns his native language in this way, whether it be English, French, or Japanese, just as the linguist elaborates a theory for any one or more of these. Of course, there are important differences between the two achievements, but neither can be explained without similar recourse to some initial and surprisingly rich hypothesis about the nature of human language. There is simply no other way to learn what we know of language.

The hypothesis of universal grammar is not first learned as such, though it can later be known, for it is rather part of what we use to learn language. We do not acquire it, because we already come with it built in as one of our original components, so to speak. Most philosophers who accept this theory would prefer to say, although few would ever admit, that universal grammar is innate. Particularly in the analytic tradition which dominates Anglo-American philosophy, opposition to almost anything innate has been a matter of principle. And Chomsky has made an effort to explain and to defend his idea of language learning and linguistic method with specific reference to philosophical objections from this intrenched camp of empiricism, most recently in his *Reflections on Language* of 1976. Actually he first drew fire, almost twenty years ago in a review[5] of B.F. Skinner's *Verbal Behavior,* with a devastating attack on behaviorism, then regarded quite favorably by philosophers and linguists as the only scientific (i.e., empirical) form of psychology. At the center of this polemic, the issues are extremely important and equally difficult to resolve, since they involve a general concept of humanity. And we are all concerned by any consensus of what we humans are in fact. As the study of mind, psychology has always been a sensitive subject dealing directly with what some consider to be the specific feature of our species, the very essence of our humanity. Transformational generative grammar has been the occasion for a new debate of this topic in this field, providing a case which could be critical and thus decisive.

On the whole, the discussion has been informative and constructive, though far from conclusive. There has been too much confusion over basic terms and claims, so that progress has rather been the type of clarification demanded for crucial concepts like knowledge when used to explain the special knowledge of language. A necessary distinction has been drawn between the "tacit" knowledge of a speaker-hearer and the more explicit knowledge of a linguist, since the former does not know the language in the exact same sense as the latter. And yet the speaker-hearer does know the language in some sense, which is more than just knowing how to speak and in this sense merely having an ability or disposition, as the empiricist thinks. The common example of chess may serve again to illustrate the difference. It is one thing to know how to play chess by knowing the rules, and surely another to know how to play skillfully. Knowledge and skill are not equivalent, even when they do coincide. And this example is closer to language than others given to refute any difference. Riding a bicycle does not require or even imply a knowledge of physics. And we are not inclined to attribute any sense of gravitation to falling apples. But the point is rather that the rules of grammar are quite different from the laws of nature, being more like conventions than instincts. These rules do not describe necessity; they define a possibility. Such rules can thus be broken, discarded, suspended, even mocked, for they are only observed when accepted, and that is how we know them.

It would probably be safe to say that many have argued, but few have convinced. And it is easy for some to conclude that such a debate could only reach a deadlock, with no hope for resolution because there are no means of solution. Like most subjects of speculation, what the mind may or may not contain is really a matter of belief rather than proof. However plausible, this sceptical and apparently neutral conclusion can hardly apply to linguistics, where it would actually prejudice the case and favor a return to empiricism. Transformational generative grammar is a definite and resolute theory of mind, requiring a realistic interpretation of linguistic competence which is to comprise first a universal and then a particular grammar firmly set in the minds of those who learn their language. Although psychologically and no doubt biologically quite real, this competence remains theoretical only in being necessarily inferred from the available evidence, which consists of intuitions about grammatical form. Moreover, it does make a practical difference in the pursuit of science by providing both reason and justification for linguistics to study more than patterns of behavior. The full difference in practice has become very clear and just as crucial again with the resurgence of empiricism within linguistics to challenge the position of transformational generative grammar.

It would be a serious mistake to suggest that the position of transformational generative grammar has not been modified since first established and defended by Chomsky more than twenty years ago. There have actually been several changes at various stages during that time. An original version of the theory appeared in *Syntactic Structures* (1957), which represented only part of a much larger work, *The Logical Structure of Linguistic Theory*, completed in 1955 but not published until 1975. A second version of the theory now known as the standard theory, was presented first by Katz and Postal in *An Integrated Theory of Linguistic Descriptions* (1964) and then by Chomsky in *Aspects of the Theory of Syntax* (1965). An extended standard theory was later proposed by Chomsky in articles collected as *Studies on Semantics in Generative Grammar* (1972). Now that last version is being revised in the very latest work. The real reason for change has simply been the type of development and refinement to be expected in any progressive science as certain formulations and approximations prove to be inadequate or inaccurate. Of course, the very fact of change does imply the occurrence of problems as well as progress. The major problem and also the major impetus for change has come with the attempt to include semantics, the study of meaning, within a full grammar along with the phonology and syntax to which it was first restricted. This problem of meaning was the cause for a schism which once divided linguistics, and it remains the source of confusion.

At first it seemed most important to prove that grammar, then restricted to phonology and syntax, was independent from meaning; and it was thus shown that a sentence could be grammatical, in the same narrow sense, without being meaningful. Examples were often chosen, like the original (1) and others such as (5), with the syntax right and the semantics wrong.

(5)   John is a happily married bachelor.

But it soon became quite obvious that if a grammar were to represent our full knowledge of English, it should contain some provision for the fact that *bachelor* means "unmarried," as we all know.

A concerted effort was then made to devise a semantic component for an enlarged grammar, where it had to be compatible with an established phonology and syntax. That is when all the trouble started—or when all the fun began! At least one thing seems certain: transformational generative grammar will never be the same. The problem with meaning is its elasticity, which also accounts for its resiliency. The already faint line between syntax and semantics was soon erased by the partisans of a generative semantics. And it was not long before the crowd for a new pragmatics, the study of language in use, would abolish all the old distinctions. Continuous revolution! they cried. Counter-revolution! the others replied. There still is some needless shouting; but again the issues are fundamental, since they go to the very foundation of linguistics: competence and performance.

Even if this type of survey did not tend to lose perspective at the edge of current work, as indeed it does, there is no way here to examine each proposal, no time now to follow every path in the study of meaning. The subject has simply become too vast (if it has not actually been lost) in all the recent effort drawing on several fields of inquiry and employing various methods of analysis. A simple list of topics under consideration may serve at least to suggest some of the diversity among those interests with a claim to insight about meaning. The following are being actively pursued: speech acts, both direct and indirect; conversational postulates and implicatures; reference and definite descriptions; proper names; natural kinds; inference and presupposition. This listing only mentions the more philosophical and says nothing of the sociological and strictly psychological perspectives on this most suggestive but quite elusive subject. Meaning itself would seem to have no single or stable meaning; and that is indeed the basic problem, both the trouble and the fun. Meaning is not limited to language alone but extends to other forms of action and intention. We may wonder about the meaning of a smile or a frown, as we may ponder the meaning of a poem. But surely all of that is not the direct concern of the linguist; he has enough to do with the original correlations of sound and meaning in language which every speaker-hearer learns and knows. And yet the issues now raised by much of the new work in semantics have had a disturbing effect on just this kind of certainty and security. The argument is simply that our full knowledge of language includes more meaning than most have been willing to admit in their transformational grammar.

Few linguists would deny that even a simple conversation requires the use of several skills and the focus of considerable knowledge, though without any conscious effort, since we can usually rely on our fluency almost the way we rely on our breathing. There are cases when we have to think twice— guessing again, repeating, or asking for an explanation—and there are even others when we give up in despair, simply unable to understand or to make ourselves understood. It seems fairly clear that we succeed in the easy cases because we know the language, but can we then say that we fail in the difficult ones because we do not know the language? There are some cases where that is literally true, but those are obviously different. Perhaps we know only English, and they speak only Hungarian. With others who also speak English we could still have difficulty, so that we may be inclined to conclude that we understand the meaning of their words but not their thoughts. We would then try to distinguish between the very meaning of a word and its possible significance, the sense it would have in a particular context. This primary meaning, or denotation, could be quite different from a secondary meaning, or connotation. It could even be opposed, as in the obvious case of irony. We can well imagine how a sentence (6) could be used to express, quite unequivocally, the reverse (7) when spoken in the proper voice.

(6) He is a genius!
(7) He is a moron.

But we would probably not be prepared to argue then that *genius* actually means "moron," in the same way that *bachelor* means "unmarried," even though we understand such meanings just as easily. Some more elaborate distinction between primary and secondary meaning is thus necessary to separate these different cases. The real problem is then to know what to do with the difference.

Theoretically at least, the original distinction between competence and performance could be applied to semantics along with phonology and syntax. Our knowledge of language as fully represented in a grammar would then include rules of semantic competence which would somehow assign meaning to sentences. And some other type of knowledge, perhaps a broadly communicative or pragmatic competence, would operate in performance, actually assigning significance to an utterance. We could thus separate our knowledge of language from our knowledge of the world at large neatly enough to maintain the integrity of linguistics. And we could then explain how a sentence (8) could be semantically anomalous and yet be used to make some utterance quite felicitous, since it would have no meaning according to the rules of competence but a perfectly acceptable, even commendable, significance in performance.

(8) Golf plays John. (Rather than the other way round!)

In practice, it is not always easy to draw the line, and there are reasons to believe that no such line can be maintained consistently throughout the field of meaning. Semantics is the area where our knowledge of language seems to encounter our general knowledge of the world with some free exchange, so that we may never be able to establish on principle any absolute difference between the dictionary for our language and the encyclopedia for all the rest of our knowledge. The entry for a common noun, like *tiger* or *lemon*, is quite arbitrary in its selection of what the language is supposed to tell us. When we actually speak, we use and indeed we need more than such cursory definitions. This none would deny. But exactly how much more it is hard to say. As a result, the trend of the new pragmatics is to discard almost every one of these distinctions, in favor of pragmantax, with the consequence that knowledge of language cannot be separated from matters of fact and belief.

Meaning would then depend solely on context. And linguistics would no longer be defined as the study of competence, since language itself would be identified with performance.

The effort within transformational generative grammar has been to hold the line on the difference between competence and performance, while making concessions about exactly how to relate syntax and semantics. Some of these concessions have been important enough to require serious revisions in the theory of syntax. And yet there remains a basic confidence in the method which has been responsible for all the success in the past. Here lies a difference in attitude so fundamental as to make it quite difficult to argue convincingly either for or against a theory when the discussion finally reaches that level. The idea of a paradigm was thought to capture that hard core of conviction which every science requires and which every scientist assumes as the basis for his work. The question may then be asked whether the paradigm in linguistics should not be changed again. Are we in need of another revolution? Those who defend transformational generative grammar surely think not, but others do. The burden of proof lies with those who argue for radical change. And what—or even how—are we to conclude? We first have to know what has to be proved, or rather what has to be removed and then replaced, for a paradigm is only disproved when thus displaced. There has to be a full alternative.

The established method would otherwise continue in a rigorously analytic manner to maintain differences and distinctions with the idea that no progress can be made in the understanding of such a complex phenomenon as human language unless the whole problem can itself be broken down into a set of smaller problems to be solved in turn. This is essentially a modular approach, not one general theory but a system of separate theories or components, more modest but perhaps more effective. It has been applied to syntax and phonology with success in the past. It has been challenged more recently in the area of semantics. And this is the situation of linguistics as it stands now. We could only guess the future. But the future is rather for you to decide.

Notes

1. Compare, for example, the introductions to Leonard Bloomfield, *Language* (New York: Holt, Rinehart & Winston, 1933) and Noam Chomsky, *Aspects of the Theory of Syntax* (Cambridge, Mass.: The M.I.T. Press, 1965)

2. See Jonathan Culler, *Saussure* (Fontana/Collins, 1976) for details.

3. See John Lyons, *Chomsky* (Fontana/Collins, 1970) for details.

4. The term comes from Thomas S. Kuhn, *The Structure of Scientific Revolutions* (The University of Chicago Press, 1962) which is the standard source and reference.

5. This now classic piece first appeared in *Language,* 35/1 (1959), pp. 26-58.

Index